Why Being Unique Makes Me Wonderful:
Children Can Learn To Understand Why They Are Unique

Written by Summer Carrillo
Illustrated by *Your Child*

Carrillo
PUBLISHING LLC

This is for Stephanie Carrillo my very unique and interesting niece, who makes me proud because she knows she is unique and she loves it. That's what makes her wonderful!

Copyright

Why Being Unique Makes Me Wonderful

Copyright © 2015, Summer Carrillo

First Printing, 2015

Published in the United States by Carrillo Publishing LLC, 2015

www.summercarrillo.com

Paperback ISBN-13: 9780692496749
Paperback ISBN-10: 0692496742

Put your picture here

I am unique

Being unique can be confusing. Sometimes it can make you experience puzzling emotions and feelings. They are a part of life. Emotions and feelings come and go like different times of the day. Every day they can change. Draw and color the times of the day in the boxes below.

Morning   Afternoon   Night

Times of the Day

Just like the times of a day, people can change how they feel too.

There will be good days.

There will be bad days.

There will be days you smile.

There will be days you laugh.

There will be days you frown.

There will be days you cry.

There will be days you are happy.

There will be days you are sad.

There will be days you are scared.

There will be days you are confident.

There will be times you sing and times you grieve!

Many Kinds of People

There are many kinds of people. They have many different kinds of personalities.

Some are quiet.

Some are loud.

Some are silly.

Some are curious.

Some are shy.

Some are confident.

Some are creative.

Some are clever.

Some are serious.

Some are playful.

When we are different, we need to learn how to get along with people.

I like Myself List

Everyone is good at something. Nobody is good at everything. It is healthy to know what you are good at and what you like. List six things you like about yourself.

1.

2.

3

I like Myself List

4.

5.

6.

Snowflakes

Shapes are unique. They are like a snowflake. No snowflake is the same. Snowflakes come in many shapes and sizes. Draw and color two creative snowflakes below.

Snowflakes

Draw and color *two more* creative snowflakes below.

Emotion Faces

When you are different, sometimes people say unkind words. Unkind words make us have emotions. Emotions help us understand what is happening inside us. No one can tell us how we are feeling; only *we* know. Draw emotion faces in the circles below.

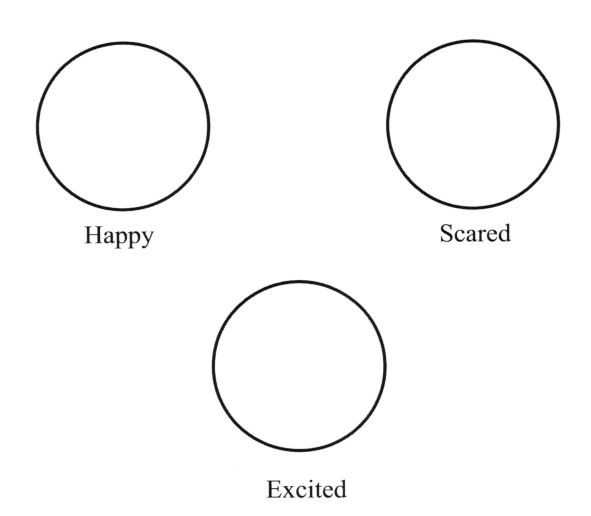

Happy

Scared

Excited

Emotion Faces

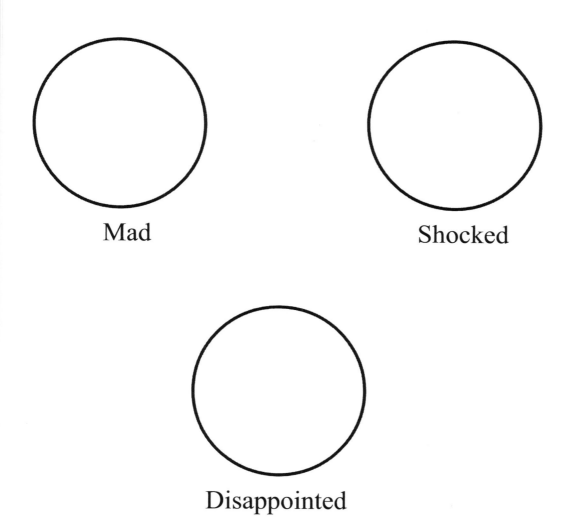

Mad

Shocked

Disappointed

Emotions and feelings are normal. They help us understand ourselves and other people.

Understanding Our Body

Emotions and feelings are something we experience in our bodies. They are called feelings because the words people use go through our skin and into our bodies. The words touch our heart and brain. This makes us *feel* an emotion. Color the heart and brain with an emotion.

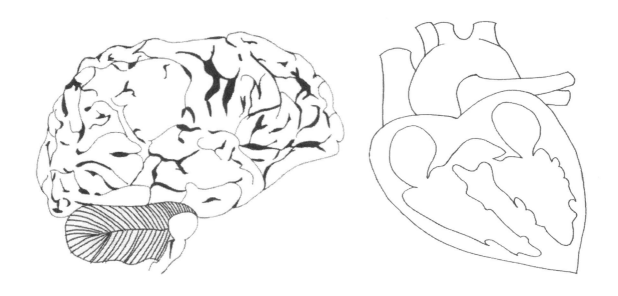

Sad—Blue
Nervous—Green
Scared—Orange
Happy—Red
Angry—Black

Feelings Across And Down

Write each of the following feeling words across and then down: Glad, Afraid, Confident, Jealous, Proud, Nervous, Happy, Joyful, Angry, Worried, Bored and Disappointed.

Example: u n i q u e
             n
             i
             q
             u
             e

Feelings Across And Down

It's okay to have emotions and feelings about being different. It's okay to talk about them too.

Feeling Pyramids

With a marker, write the kind words in a pyramid. With a crayon put an X over the mean words.

An example of a pyramid word:

```
      H
     HA
    HAP
   HAPP
  HAPPY
```

Feeling Pyramids

Unique	Weird	Remarkable
Interesting	Wonderful	Strange
Special	Odd	Valuable

Feeling Vowels And Consonants

Look at the beginning letter of each word. Write the words under the correct heading.

Afraid   Nervous   Confident   Excited

Upset   Interested   Angry   Eager

Jealous   Bored   Courage   Brave

Curious   Overwhelmed

VOWELS	CONSONANTS
1.	1. Brave
2.	2.
3.	3.
4.	4.
5.	5.
6.	6.
7.	7.

Accept Your Feelings

It is all right to say to yourself: "I am afraid." "I am embarrassed." "I am confused." "I am nervous." It is good to know how you feel. When you understand how you feel, it's called "accepting." When you accept your feelings, you can find a *healthy* way to work through a problem. It is important to know how you feel so you can think about *smart* ways to help yourself.

Yesterday at (place)_____ I felt

_____.

Today at (place)_____

I was feeling_____.

Tomorrow when I'm at (place)_____

I want to feel _____.

Working Through Bad Feelings and Emotions

Sometimes people think that because we can't see feelings, they are not real. When bad emotions are stuck in our bodies, we get sick. Sometimes we have aches and pains; other times we get tired and lazy. If bad emotions and feelings are stuck inside too long we have a hard time eating and sleeping. Good ways to let feelings out are…

1. Drawing
2. Laughing
3. Playing Music
4. Playing
5. Singing
6. Writing
7. Exercising
8. Creating Art
9. Crying
10. Playing Sports
11. Talking
12. Running

Being unique can be <u>fun</u> and <u>scary</u>. Sometimes I feel scared because…

The <u>fun</u> things about <u>me</u> are…..

It's okay for you to be different! It's okay to be afraid when you are not the same.

You Are A Gift

Being unique is a gift. You are a gift. Color, draw, and create a present that is unique like you….

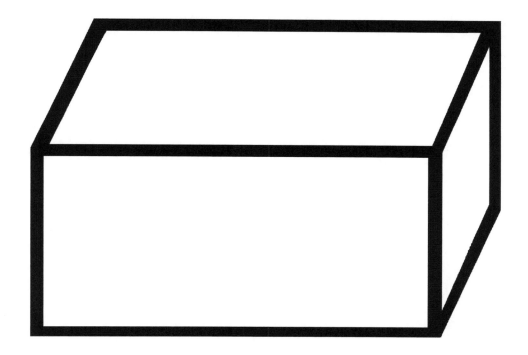

Unique

Things You Are Good At

I am special because I am unique. *Remember*, everyone is good at something. Nobody is good at everything. This is why we are unique. Draw some things that you are good at.

Communicating With Your Family

Families are important. We spend so much time with our families. Families may have problems when they are not communicating. Communicating means showing how you feel. List five ways that show how you can communicate with your family.

1.

2.

3.

4.

5.

Understanding How Your Parents Show Their Feelings

It's okay for you to have emotions and feelings around your family. We learn from our parents how to act when we are happy, sad, mad, or scared. Draw a picture of what your parents do when they are …

Happy

Sad

Understanding How Your Parents Show Their Feelings

Mad

Scared

Emotions and feelings can change the way you act or say things. It is important to understand how your mom and your dad act when they are happy, sad, mad or scared.

Family Tree

Families are like trees. Every person in a family is important. They are all connected to each other, just like branches on a tree. If one person is hurt, it affects everyone in the family. Place each feeling word in one of the branches of the tree.

Joyful   Stressed   Confident   Angry   Excited

Sad   Jealous   Proud   Upset   Afraid

Family Tree

Characters Within A Family

Each person in a family is like a character in a play. Sometimes, a character can play more than one role. We are not worried when we know how each character will act; but when someone in our family changes, the family may become unbalanced. Name each person on the stage.

Perfect Person   Funny Person   Problem Person

Person who helps and
listens to the family

Shy person

Smart
Person

Person who solves problems

Bad Ways To Show Feelings

Sometimes people think boys and girls do not have the same feelings and emotions. This is because someone *taught* them that some feelings are bad. This is *learned* from T.V. shows, friends, or family members. They are taught to be *afraid* to use *their words* to show their feelings. Boys and girls are *not* different. They have the *same* feelings. Everyone has them. Just like there are good ways to show feelings, there are bad ways too. Bad ways to let feelings out are…

1. Yelling

2. Hitting

3. Lying

4. Biting

5. Kicking

6. Gossiping

7. Saying mean words

8. Throwing stuff

9. Ignoring people

10. Hurting yourself

Emotions and feelings are healthy and normal. It is the way you show your feelings and emotions that makes it right or wrong.

Unkind Words

There are people who might not understand that you are unique. This can make you feel embarrassed or uncomfortable. They may use unkind words that can hurt your feelings. Circle the unkind words with a blue marker in each sentence.

- Says I am weird

- Tells me I am strange

- Tells others I am crazy

- Tells me my ideas are stupid

- Says mean jokes about me

- Tells me that I am odd

When people don't understand, they can be mean. This is because they are *scared* you are different from them so they say unkind things.

Showing Support

Other times a family might support you when you are unique. This will make you feel loved and proud to be different. Some things they can do to make you feel good are…

1. Thank me when I do something special for them.

2. Ask me how I feel when I do something unique.

3. Helping me find things that I find interesting.

4. Give me a chance to make choices.

5. Compliments me on good decisions I make.

6. Encourages me to trust myself when I try something different.

Being different makes you interesting!

Sometimes a family does not know how to show you that being different is natural and a good thing. They do not show that they care about what you like. What are some things you like to do that are special?

I like to do…..

Decoding Sentences
Use the vowels to finish each sentence A E I O U.

I __m

__ n __q __ __.

I __m

s p__ c __ __l.

Decoding Sentences

I __m

__

g __f t.

I __m

__ n t __ r __ s t __ n g.

Social Support System

When you are around people who care about you, they are called your social support. It's okay to ask your social support for help. Many people care about me because I am valuable. I feel comfortable talking about my emotions and feelings with people I trust will support and guide me. This is a list that names people I trust. I can ask them for help.

1. Parent name(s)_____

2. Grandparent name(s)_____

3. Name of a relative(s)_____

4. Name of a friend(s) _____

5. Name of a teacher _____

Social Support System

6. Name of a counselor _____

7. Name of a neighbor(s)_____

8. Name of a school nurse_____

9. Name of a doctor _____

10. Name of a church _____

11. Emergency number(s)_____

I Am Me

I am *ME*. I can be UNIQUE, be ME, and be HAPPY!

This is a picture of me happy….

Being different is a natural part of life. Be proud you are (name) _____. It's what makes you WONDERFUL.

Printed in Great Britain
by Amazon

Instruction Book

McCormick-Deering
FARMALL TRACTOR
Model F-30

With Sectional Views and Parts List

MANUFACTURED BY

INTERNATIONAL HARVESTER COMPANY
(INCORPORATED)

606 So. MICHIGAN AVE.   CHICAGO, U. S. A.

SPECIFICATIONS

Engine

Bore. . . . .$4\frac{1}{4}''$

Stroke. . . . .$5''$

Engine speed. . . . . .1150 r. p. m.

Pulley speed. . . . . .682 r. p. m.

Belt speed. . . . . .2612 ft. p. m.

Power take-off shaft speed. . . . . .534 r. p. m.

Pulley diameter. . . . .$14\frac{5}{8}''$

Pulley face. . . . .$7''$

Kerosene tank. . . . . .21 gals.

Gas tank. . . . . .1 gal.

Water cooling system (capacity). . . . . .Approx. 10 gals.

Clutch

Single plate dry disk. . . . . .12 in.

Transmission (Four-Speed)

Forward speed, miles per hour. . . . . .2, $2\frac{3}{4}$, $3\frac{1}{4}$ and $3\frac{3}{4}$

Reverse speed, miles per hour. . . . .$2\frac{1}{2}$

Wheels

Front wheel. . . . . .4 x 25 in.

Drive wheel. . . . . .12 x 42 in.

Tread, front. . . . .$9\frac{3}{8}$ in.

Tread, rear. . . . . .77 in.

Wheelbase. . . . . .94 in.

Skid ring. . . . . 2 in.

Lugs (spade). . . . . 5 in.

General

Length (over all). . . . . .147 in.

Width (over all). . . . .$89\frac{1}{4}$ in.

Total height—steering wheel. . . . .$70\frac{1}{2}$ in.

Total height—radiator. . . . .$64\frac{11}{16}$ in.

Turning radius . . . . .8 ft., 8 in.

ERRATA

Instruction Book Farmall "F-30" (McD-3060)

The following corrections should be made:

Page 61, Item Ref.No.2- Part No.19175D should read 19175C

    "   67,   "   "   " 8-   "   "   13570D   "   "   13870D

    "   ",   "   "   " 31-   "   "   16552D   "   "   16852D

    "   ",   "   "   " 43-   "   "   D7323   "   "   D7147

    "   ",   "   "   " 46-   "   "   12335D   "   "   12435D

    "   87,   "   "   " 21-   "   "   10862H   "   "   10862D

STARTING, OPERATING, LUBRICATION, GENERAL

INDEX

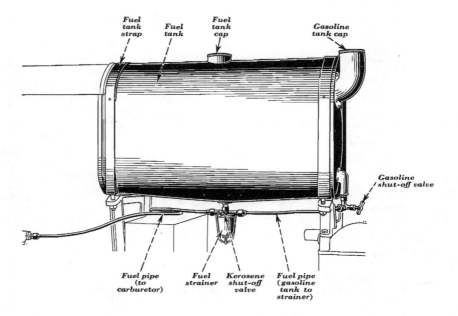

Illustration No. 1
Fuel tanks, tank connections, shut-off needle valves, fuel strainer, etc.

PRELIMINARY INSTRUCTIONS

Examine the tractor carefully and see that all oil holes are cleaned of paint and dirt—if any threaded oil holes are found and there are no connections, look at the oiling diagram. If connection is shown, and not in place, it was probably lost in transit and should be replaced before starting up.

> To assist in maintaining proper operation of engine, refer to the "CORRECTIVE MEASURES" on pages 39, 40 and 41.

Preparations for Starting

Close kerosene and gasoline shut-off needle valves. *(See illustration No. 1.)*

Fill fuel tank with clean kerosene (capacity 21 gallons). *(See illustration No. 1.)*

Fill gasoline tank with gasoline (capacity 1 gallon). *(See illustration No. 1.)*

Carefully strain all fuel and be sure it is free from water.

Gasoline is necessary only when starting and warming up the engine.

Fill radiator with *clean* water within *3 inches* of the top and keep it well filled. Soft or rain water should be used if it can be readily obtained.

Pull up radiator curtain to top of radiator.
(See special instructions on page 35.)

See that the engine has the proper amount of oil in the crankcase. *(See illustration No. 6.)*

See that all lubrication connections are filled with lubricant approved for use in Alemite-Zerk compressor. *(See Specifications on page 13.)*

See that oil in transmission is up to level of plug located in front of transmission case. *(See "Lubrication Chart," illustration No. 9.)*

See that oil in rear axle carrier is up to level of plug located on side of carrier. *(See "Lubrication Chart," illustration No. 9.)*

See that oil in steering gear case is up to level of plug located on side of case. *(See "Lubrication Chart," illustration No. 9.)*

See that oil in oil air filter is up to proper level. *(See illustration No. 14.)*

Tractors shipped Domestic and Canada have a supply of oil in all parts. All oil has been drained from tractors shipped Export.

Complete instructions for oiling are shown on "Lubrication Chart." (See pages 10 to 12.)

Special Precautions with a New Engine

Before starting a new engine, remove the spark plugs and put about one ounce of gas engine lubricating oil into each cylinder, replace the spark plugs and crank the engine to distribute the oil over the cylinder walls.

During the first one hundred hours of operation, mix one pint of engine oil with every five gallons of fuel.

Never run a new engine immediately under full load. Work it easily until you are sure that oil has reached all parts.

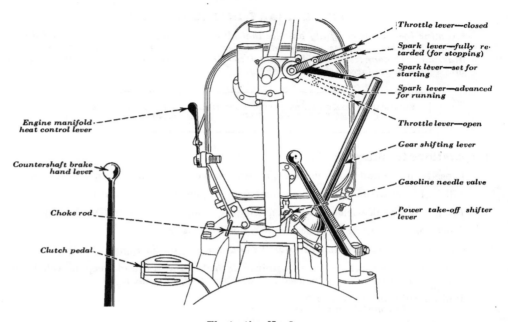

Throttle lever—closed

Spark lever—fully re-tarded (for stopping)

Spark lever—set for starting

Spark lever—advanced for running

Throttle lever—open

Gear shifting lever

Gasoline needle valve

Power take-off shifter lever

Engine manifold heat control lever

Countershaft brake hand lever

Choke rod

Clutch pedal

Illustration No. 2

Rear view, showing controls.

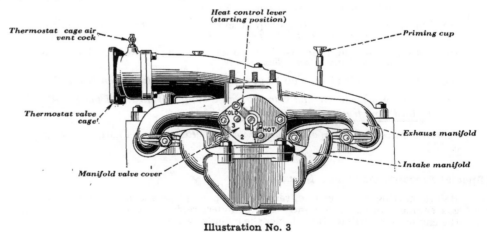

Heat control lever (starting position)

Priming cup

Thermostat cage air vent cock

Thermostat valve cage

Exhaust manifold

Intake manifold

Manifold valve cover

COLD

HOT

3

2

Illustration No. 3

Detail of heat control, manifold, etc.

Before Starting Engine

Put gear shifting lever in neutral position. *(See illustrations Nos. 2 and 7.)*

Open throttle lever by moving lever down. *(See illustration No. 2.)*

Open gasoline shut-off needle valve. *(See illustration No. 1.)*

The heat control lever (located on left side of fuel tank) should be pushed forward all the way, setting heat control on engine manifold to **"Hot"** or "No. 1" position. *(See illustrations Nos. 2 and 3.)*

To Start Engine

Prime cylinders with gasoline through priming cups. *(See illustration No. 3.)*

With spark lever fully retarded and the choker valve completely closed, crank engine rapidly three or four revolutions. Then move spark lever to starting position *(see illustration No. 2)*, move choker valve nearly one-half open and crank engine.

As soon as engine starts, the choker valve should be opened to where the engine runs without missing.

Note: Should the engine be started with the spark lever all the way down (fully advanced), there is danger of a "back-fire" or "kick" which may injure the operator.

After Engine Starts and Is Warmed Up

Engine should warm up in from five to eight minutes.

Spark and throttle control levers must be adjusted for proper advance for load to be handled. *(See illustration No. 2.)*

After *gasoline* shut-off needle valve has been *closed tight*, quickly open *kerosene* shut-off needle valve, but *never have both valves open or even partly open at the same time*, otherwise kerosene will mix with gasoline, making it unsatisfactory for starting. *(See illustration No. 1.)*

Set Heat Control Valve after Engine Warms Up

When operating on kerosene, the valve on engine manifold should be set so that the indicator points to **"Hot"** or "No. 1" on the cover plate. *(See illustration No. 3.)*

When operating on gasoline, start with valve on **"Hot"** or "No. 1" position. After engine is thoroughly warmed up, the indicator should be set at **"Cold"** or "No. 3" position. In extremely cold weather or when operating under light load, the heat control valve should be set at **"Intermediate"** or "No. 2" position.

It is important that control valve be properly set to correspond with the fuel being used. *(See illustrations Nos. 2 and 3, and instructions on page 9.)*

6

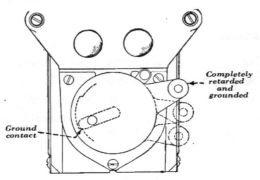

Illustration No. 4—International E4A Magneto.

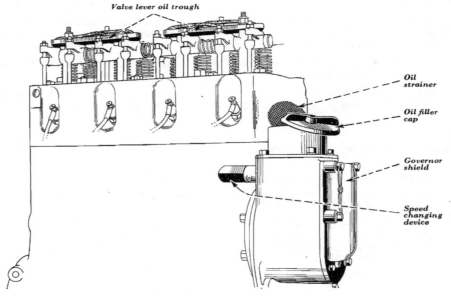

Illustration No. 5—Crankcase oil filler, governor, etc.

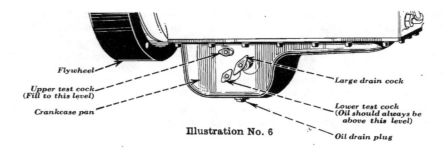

Illustration No. 6

To Start Tractor

Place left foot on clutch pedal and press down firmly, holding in this position; this disengages the clutch. *Clutch must always be disengaged while shifting gears.* *(See illustration No. 2.)*

Move gear shifting lever to required position. *(See illustrations Nos. 2 and 7, and instructions below.)*

Gently release pressure on clutch pedal; this engages clutch and causes tractor to move. *(See illustration No. 2.)*

Gear Shifting

Always disengage clutch before making a gear shift.

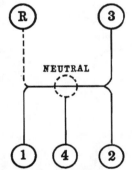

Illustration No. 7
Showing different positions
of gear shifting lever.

Neutral...................hand lever in a vertical position.
1. **Low speed forward**........move hand lever to left and back.
2. **Intermediate speed forward.**move hand lever to right and back.
3. **Third speed forward**.......move hand lever to right and forward.
4. **High speed forward**........move hand lever straight back from neutral.
R. **Reverse**..................move hand lever to left and forward.

To Stop Tractor

Disengage clutch.

Press down firmly on clutch pedal, then move gear shifting lever to neutral position *(See illustrations Nos. 2 and 7.)*

To Stop Engine

Close *kerosene* shut-off needle valve and open *gasoline* needle valve just long enough to fill the strainer with gasoline. Then close the needle valve and run engine until all kerosene is used out of carburetor and fuel pipe, in order to insure having gasoline in the fuel bowl when starting up again. *(See illustration No. 1.)*

The automatic grounding switch on the magneto should be used only in emergencies, when the engine must be stopped quickly. *(See illustration No. 4.)*

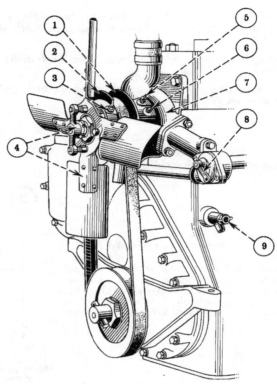

Illustration No. 8

Fan and water pump assembly.

Ref. No.	DESCRIPTION
1	Fan pulley.
2	Fan pulley flange.
3	Fan pulley set screw.
4	Fan assembly.
5	Fan hub bearing lubricator.
6	Water pump shaft lubricator.
7	Water pump body.
8	Throttle connecting rod arm.
9	Crankcase water drain cock.

Operation of Heat Control

Built into the exhaust and intake manifold is a rotary valve which controls the exhaust gas passageway. This valve is controllable from the operator's seat and enables the operator to turn all the exhaust gas heat around, or divert all heat from, the intake manifold. The manifold is plainly marked and has three positions noted for this valve. (*See illustration No. 3.*)

Position **1** is "Hot," Position **3** is "Cold," and Position **2** is between the two. Position 1 should *always* be used when starting the engine and during the warming-up period. *This is true whether using gasoline or kerosene.* When using gasoline all the time, it will be desirable to move this valve to Position 3 very shortly after starting engine, depending on the weather and load. When starting on gasoline and operating on kerosene, it will be desirable to keep the valve in Position 1 most of the time unless the weather is hot. In hot weather with a heavy load on the engine, good results may be obtained with this valve in Position 3, but generally, better results will be secured if the intake manifold is kept hot when using kerosene. To secure this condition and not sacrifice too much power, it will be desirable to set valve at Position 2. If not kept hot, fuel will not be properly vaporized and dilution of the crankcase lubricating oil as well as imperfect regulation of engine will result.

Shut-off Needle Valves

The shut-off needle valves for gasoline and kerosene should always be closed when engine is stopped for more than an hour. (*See illustration No. 1.*)

Fuel Strainer

The fuel strainer should be taken apart and cleaned at least once a week when tractor is in use. This is done by first closing all shut-off needle valves for the gasoline and kerosene tanks. (*See illustration No. 1.*)

To take strainer apart, loosen the lower jam nut, then the bowl adjusting nut, and swing the bail wire to one side. Fuel bowl and wire screen can then be lowererd removed and cleaned. If screen is not corroded or clogged, it will not be necessay, to remove it.

In reassembling the fuel strainer, be sure that cork gasket between the bowl and main body is in good condition and does not leak.

Water System

The cooling of the engine is accomplished by a water circulating pump having a thermostatic control valve. The water level must not be allowed to drop below the radiator inlet, otherwise the loss of water will be excessive and the engine will overheat. (*See further instructions on page 27.*)

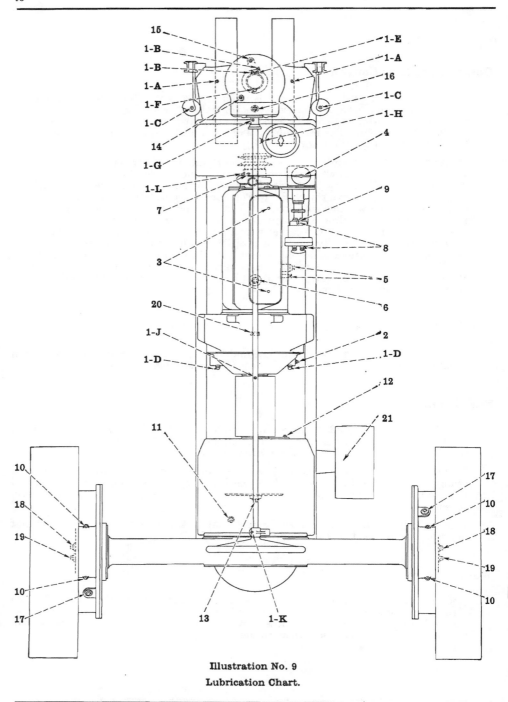

Illustration No. 9
Lubrication Chart.

KEY TO LUBRICATION CHART

(See illustration No. 9)

1	**A**—Front wheel bearing............ **B**—Front axle shaft bearing.......... **C**—Countershaft brake sheave........ **D**—Clutch shifter shaft bearing....... **E**—Countershaft brake lever......... **F**—Front axle shaft spacer............ **G**—Steering spur pinion bearing....... **H**—Starting crank bearing........... **J**—Clutch shaft ball bearing.......... **K**—Steering shaft bearing, rear.......	Daily. Use approved lubricant.
	L—Water pump shaft (bottom fitting)..	Daily. Use approved lubricant. Not over two pumps of gun. **Note:** Over-lubrication of the water pump shaft will cause lubricant to be forced into the water system and cause serious trouble. *Do not over-lubricate.*
2	Clutch release bearing................	Daily. About 5 or 6 complete strokes of the compressor. Use approved lubricant.
3	Valve lever oil trough...............	Daily. Use cylinder oil. One-sixth of oil can as furnished with tractor.
4	Crankcase........................ (Oil filler)	Drain crankcase down to large drain cock and refill with fresh oil to level of upper test cock after every 10 hours' run. Drain all oil from crankcase pan once every 60 hours' run, and refill with fresh oil. Use S.A.E. No. 20 or No. 30 oil for cold or cool weather and S.A.E. No. 40 or No. 50 oil for warm or hot weather.
5	Crankcase........................ (Oil drain cocks)	Proper oil level in crankcase pan.
6	Crankcase pan oil drain plug...	
7	Fan hub bearing (top fitting).........	Once per week. Use approved lubricant. Two pumps of the gun. **Note:** If lubricant oozes out of the fan hub while using the Zerk gun, it indicates excess lubrication. *Do not over-lubricate.*
8	Magneto..........................	Once a week. Few drops of sewing machine oil or cream separator oil. *(See other instructions on pages 20 to 23.)*
9	Impulse coupling....................	Once a week remove cover and oil liberally with cream separator oil. *(See other instructions on pages 20 to 23.)*
10	Countershaft brake camshaft.......... Countershaft brake shoe pin...........	Once a week; a few drops of cylinder oil.
11	Transmission...................... (Oil filler plug)	Use approved lubricant. Keep lubricant in transmission up to level of plug **(12)** which indicates the proper oil level. (Transmission holds approximately 7 gallons of lubricant.)
12	Transmission...................... (Oil level plug)	Proper oil level in transmission.

(Continued on next page)

☞*Specifications for approved lubricant are shown on page 13.*

12

KEY TO LUBRICATION CHART—Continued

(See illustration No. 9)

13	Transmission oil drain plug...	
14	Steering gear case................... (Oil filler plug)	Use approved lubricant. Keep lubricant up to level of plug **(15)** placed on side of gear case. (Steering gear case holds approximately 1 quart of lubricant.)
15	Steering gear case................... (Oil level plug)	Proper oil level in gear case.
16	Steering gear case drain plug...	
17	Rear axle carrier.................... (Oil filler plug)	Use approved lubricant. Keep lubricant up to level of plug **(18)** placed on side of carrier. (Rear axle carrier holds approximately ½ gallon of lubricant.)
18	Rear axle carrier.................... (Oil level plug)	Proper oil level in rear axle carrier.
19	Rear axle carrier oil drain plug......................................	
20	Clutch shaft pilot bearing.............	Automatically lubricated from crankshaft.
21	Belt pulley drive shaft................ (Bearings)	Automatically lubricated from transmission case.

☞*Specifications for approved lubricant are shown on page 13.*

Transmission, Rear Axle and Steering Case Lubrication

When the tractor is shipped from the factory to points in the United States and Canada the transmission, rear axle carrier and steering case are filled to proper level with an approved lubricant.

Tractors packed and shipped Export have had all oil drained before shipment, and before attempting to operate, transmission case, rear axle carrier and steering case must be filled to proper level with an approved lubricant.

See "Lubrication Chart" (illustration No. 9), also Specifications covering Approved Transmission Lubricant (page 13).

Oil should be inspected monthly and kept up to the proper level.

The transmission and final gears including differential and all bearings for the transmission are oiled automatically. The transmission and rear axle housing is filled to a definite level with heavy lubricant and the rotation of the gears splashes this to all points. The gearings and bearings which drive the belt pulley are also oiled from this same splashing. Attention need be given these only when supply of lubricant is too low, or in case of some accident.

It should not be necessary to add lubricant to transmission oftener than once a season unless excessive leakage occurs somewhere, or in case of accident, causing loss of grease.

Use approved transmission lubricant. Keep the lubricant up to level of plug located in the front of the transmission case. Oil must be such as to remain fluid in cold weather. If it does not, change should be made so proper lubrication will be effected. Oil that is up to specifications will be satisfactory for all seasons and normal operating temperatures. Special effort should be made to obtain the correct oil. (*See page 13 for lubrication specifications.*)

ALEMITE "PUSH TYPE" LUBRICATION SYSTEM

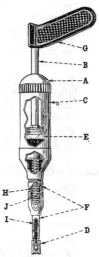

Illustration No. 10
Alemite "Push Type"
Compressor.

Filling the Compressor

Remove plunger assembly "B" by unscrewing cap "A" and fill barrel "C" to within ½" of the top with approved lubricant, as specified below. Spread the leather washer "F" and replace the plunger assembly "B." Press the nozzle "D" against some solid object and push on handle "G" with quick strokes until the lubricant starts to come out at "D". *(See illustration No. 10.)*

Instructions for Lubricating

Wipe all dirt from fittings and, with the compressor as nearly in a straight line with the fitting opening as possible, actuate handle "G" until lubricant starts to squeeze out of bearing. (Do not twist handle when operating the compressor.) **Warning**! Lubricant container should always be covered to prevent the entry of dirt.

Approved lubricant for use in Alemite "Push Type" Compressor
Transmission, Differential, Steering Gear, etc.

Oil used under this specification must be properly refined petroleum oil. It shall not contain grit, sediment, acid, alkali, soap, resin, excessive moisture or any substance not derived from petroleum.

The flashing point, Cleveland open cup, shall not be below 350° F.

The viscosity, Saybolt Universal, at 210° F. shall be between 140-150 Sec.

Lubricant shall have a cold test 0° F.   A.S.T.M. method of testing.

Pour test shall be 5° F. plus, higher than cold test.

The water and sediment shall not exceed 0.5% by volume.

The lubricant shall not corrode any metal used in the construction of the machine.

Engine Lubrication

The life and efficient working of the engine depends on proper lubrication; neglect in this direction may cause serious trouble, excessive wear and complete breakdown Properly oiled working parts must always have a thin film of oil between them; the kind of oil to use under a given condition is determined by its ability to establish this film between the rubbing parts, and to resist being squeezed out under normal pressure. It must also be of proper quality to resist decomposition caused by heat. The average operator does not know that to get the maximum horse power from his tractor he must look after his lubricating oil as closely as he does his fuel. The best oil that can be obtained will wear out and become gritty in time.

Too much cannot be said about the need of good oil of the proper body. Oil which is suitable for lubrication of internal combustion engines must be *neutral*—that is, free from *acid or alkali* reaction; free from moisture, tarry or suspended matter; must have no thickeners or mineral in suspension.

SAE No. 20 or No. 30 oil should be used in cold or cool weather and SAE No. 40 or No. 50 oil in warm or hot weather.

Engine Oiling Instructions

Engine oiling is very important and instructions should be followed closely. The oil should be drained down to the level of the *large drain cock* located on the right side of the crankcase pan and replenished with fresh oil to the level of the *top test cock*, after every 10 hours of work.

Drain the engine oil completely after every 60 hours' run *except when tractors are operating in very dusty or extremely dry soil, in which case the oil in the crankcase should be completely changed more often; at least once a day if necessary.* Remove the drain plug, located in the bottom of the crankcase sump for this purpose. (*See illustration No. 6.*) In cold weather drain all oil from crankcase pan when engine is shut down for the night, or a longer period. This should be done while the oil is hot so it will drain freely and completely. When refilling, warm oil *thoroughly* and pour into crankcase just before starting the engine as this will insure oil thin enough to pass through screen over pump suction, as with very cold oil it is possible to have lots of oil above the screen and none below for the pump to handle. The oil strainer in governor housing should be removed occasionally and cleaned.

Engine Oiling System

Cylinders, connecting rods, crankshaft bearings, camshaft, and all parts within the crankcase are lubricated by splash.

Engine Oil Supply

The oil must be poured into the crankcase sump through an opening for this purpose located on the governor housing at the front of the engine. If poured in through the hand holes, governor parts will not be sufficiently lubricated. Two small test cocks are located on the right side of the crankcase pan which indicate the high and low level of the oil. The oil should never be above the high level nor below the low level. (*See illustration No. 6.*)

Oil Pressure Gauge

The indicator pointer in oil pressure gauge should register at all times when the engine is running. Should the gauge not register, it is an indication that the oil pump is not performing properly or the oil supply needs renewing. The engine should be stopped immediately and the oil system inspected to find the cause of failure.

Cleaning the Oil Filter

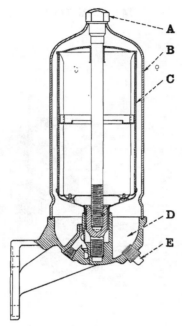

Illustration No. 11
Sectional detail of oil filter (Purolator) (20682DX).

1. Stop engine.

2. Remove drain plug "E" and drain the oil filter, replacing plug *tight.*

3. Unscrew bolt "A" until it is free.

4. Lift shell "B" up to edge of hood.

5. Holding shell up with right hand, lift element "C" up from base with left hand. Tilt both outward and remove.

6. Draw out bolt and remove element from shell.

7. Wash element in clean fuel, using soft brush or cloth.

8. Drain element when clean and replace into shell, then replace bolt. Hold element in shell, and replace on base "D."

9. Start bolt "A" by hand and draw down with wrench until oil tight.

Note: The metal filter should be cleaned *each time the engine oil is changed.*

CARBURETOR

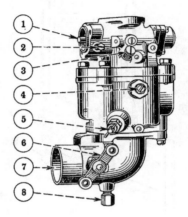

Illustration No. 12

Zenith carburetor, Model K-5 (20590D).

Ref. No.	DESCRIPTION
1	Throttle shaft.
2	Throttle plate adjusting screw.
3	Idling needle valve.
4	Main jet adjustment.
5	Drain plug.
6	Air shutter plate lever.
7	Air intake.
8	Drip plug.

Carburetor (Zenith Model K-5)
(See illustration No. 12.)

The Zenith Model K-5 Carburetor, used on this tractor, is especially developed for this equipment. It is fully balanced for use with the International oil air filter. The fuel for all but idling operation is delivered to the diffuser through two jets, the main and supplement jets. In combination, these jets deliver fuel for an average mixture of correct proportions. The proper amount of air is measured by the venturi. For idling, the fuel is fed through this idling jet.

Idling Adjustment

Do not expect a new engine that is too stiff to "rock" on compression when stopped, to idle well at low speed. Set stop screw on throttle lever so that engine will run sufficiently fast to keep it from stalling. Turn in or out on idling needle valve, until engine hits evenly and without rolling or skipping. Then back off on stop screw until desired engine speed is obtained. During the latter operation it sometimes happens that the idling needle valve can be opened a trifle, as the nearer the throttle plate is to the closed position, the greater the suction on the idling jet.

The correct idling adjustment is usually found between 1 and 3 turns open of the idling needle valve. A good starting point is $1\frac{1}{2}$ turns from its seat.

Main Jet Adjustment

To regulate main jet adjustment, retard the spark and open the throttle to approximately $\frac{1}{4}$ open and turn the adjustment clockwise, shutting off the fuel so the R.P.M. of the engine drops because of lean mixture; then open the adjustment until the R.P.M. drops because of a rich mixture, then turn back halfway between these two points to where the R.P.M. of the engine is the highest.

Fuel Level

The fuel level on the K-5 Carburetor is measured from the top edge of the fuel bowl. The correct level should be between $\frac{13}{32}''$ and $\frac{27}{64}''$ from this edge. Fuel valve seat assemblies are interchangeable.

Note: Do not bend the float hinge to change the fuel level.

Care of Carburetor

About the only thing that can disturb the functioning of the carburetor is the presence of dirt and water. Accordingly, it should be cleaned periodically, as this will insure uninterrupted operation. The fuel screen is removed by unscrewing the filter plug, *as shown in illustration No. 12A.*

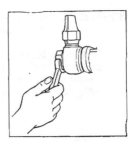

Illustration No. 12A

Governor

The rated or governed speed is 1150 R. P. M. for full load, which gives an idle speed of approximately 1275 R. P. M.

The governor is provided with a speed changing device which allows the engine speed to be decreased approximately 200 R. P. M.

This device is located in back of the governor housing and speed can be decreased by turning block to the left.
(*See illustration No. 5.*)

This device will be found useful in obtaining proper speeds quickly when tractor is operating threshers and similar machines requiring close speed regulation.

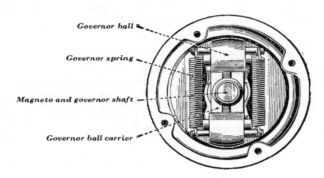

Governor ball

Governor spring

Magneto and governor shaft

Governor ball carrier

Illustration No. 13
Governor detail.

Throttle Lever
(*See illustration No. 2.*)

The rear lever located under the steering wheel is the throttle lever. Since the governor maintains constant engine speed under variable loads, this lever should be used only to reduce the speed of the engine below normal operating speed, at which very little load can be handled by the engine.

AIR FILTERING SYSTEM

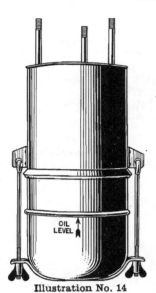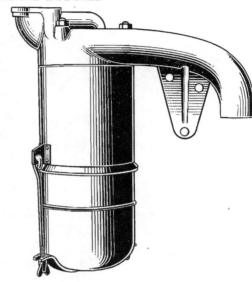

Illustration No. 14   Illustration No. 15

The engine is equipped with an International Oil Air Filter.

Air Pipe Screen

The air intake pipe is provided with a screen to prevent large particles of matter from entering the air cleaner. Keep this screen clean, as water or oil on it may catch sufficient dust to restrict the air flow to the motor.

Air Filter

After passing through the air pipe screen and the air pipe, the air passes through the air filter where the fine dust particles are removed before the air enters the engine. The air filter will function properly only when given regular attention and servicing.

The oil cup must be filled to the indicated level with a light oil before starting the engine. Drained crankcase oil is satisfactory; however, in hot weather the dilutes may be evaporated and oil should be added to keep the oil up to the indicated level.

Care of Air Filter

Remove the air filter oil cup daily and observe the oil level and refill to indicated level if there has been any evaporation. Clean out the cup and refill at least every thirty hours and when operating under very dusty conditions, clean it out and refill more often.

It is important to remove the entire air filter occasionally and wash it thoroughly. To do so, remove the oil cup and the nuts at the top of the casting, taking care not to injure the copper gasket when separating the air filter from the top casting. Remove the bottom plate (held in place by three screws) and pour gasoline or kerosene through from the top. Before replacing, be sure to replace the bottom plate and gasket. Clean the air pipe occasionally. Keep the clamps on rubber hose leading to carburetor tight, and renew the hose connections before they have rotted out.

Oil Recommended for Air Filter

At temperature above 40° (Fahrenheit), use oil drained from crankcase.

At 40° to 10° above zero (Fahrenheit), use four parts drained crankcase oil and one part kerosene.

At 10° above zero (Fahrenheit) or colder, use one part drained crankcase oil and one part kerosene.

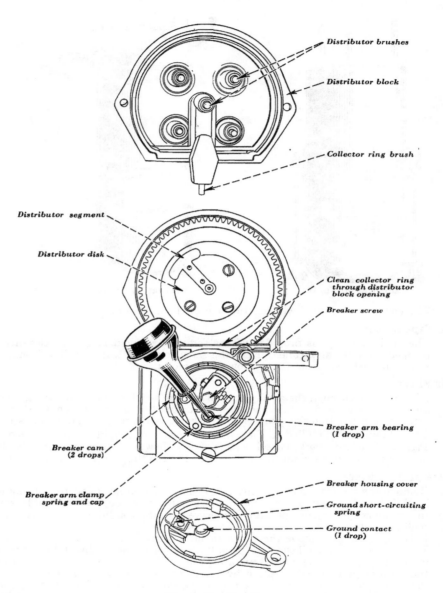

Distributor brushes

Distributor block

Collector ring brush

Distributor segment

Distributor disk

Clean collector ring through distributor block opening

Breaker screw

Breaker arm bearing (1 drop)

Breaker cam (2 drops)

Breaker arm clamp spring and cap

Breaker housing cover

Ground short-circuiting spring

Ground contact (1 drop)

Illustration No. 16
Detail of magneto.

IGNITION SYSTEM

The engine is equipped with the International E4A Magneto and the International Automatic Impulse Starter Coupling.

Magneto and Impulse Coupling—Lubrication

Important! When the engine is first received, or when it has stood idle for more than three months, both armature and distributor gear bearing oil holes should be filled twice and the impulse coupling liberally oiled, before starting the engine.

After every fifty hours of operation, lubricate the following places with cream separator or sewing machine oil:

> Armature bearings..............two drops in each cup.
> Distributor gear bearing.........five drops.
> (*) Impulse coupling...........twenty drops (at least one spoonful).

> (*)Squirt in forcibly at least 3 or 4 shots from a full oil can, also oil the pawl pins and hook on clutch plate. The impulse coupling cannot be over-oiled. (*See illustration No. 17.*)

After every 200 to 300 hours of operation, lubricate the following places with cream separator or sewing machine oil:

> Ground contact................one drop.
> Breaker screw..................one drop.
> Breaker cam...................two drops of oil in the small felt under the breaker cam.
> Breaker arm bearing...........one drop.

Crank the engine so that the hollow pivot bearing is at the bottom of the breaker housing, to prevent oil from dripping on the breaker points. With the fingers lift up the breaker arm clamp spring and cap which covers the hollow pivot bearing, swing it to one side, and put one drop of oil in the opening. (*See illustration No. 16.*)

Warning! *Do not oil the magneto more than specified and do not use heavier oil than specified,* as it will gum the working parts of the magneto and make the impulse coupling inoperative, which may cause the engine to "kick back" when being cranked, resulting in serious injury to the operator, if the spark is not retarded.

22

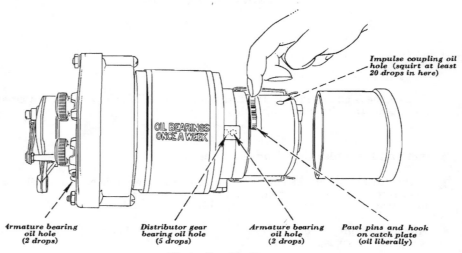

Impulse coupling oil
hole (squirt at least
20 drops in here)

OIL BEARINGS
ONCE A WEEK

Armature bearing
oil hole
(2 drops)

Distributor gear
bearing oil hole
(5 drops)

Armature bearing
oil hole
(2 drops)

Pawl pins and hook
on catch plate
(oil liberally)

Illustration No. 17

Top view of magneto.

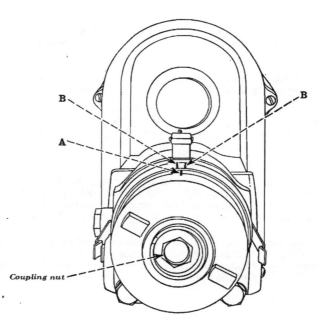

B

B

A

Coupling nut

Illustration No. 18

Impulse coupling, showing timing marks.

Circuit Breaker

The breaker point opening should be from .012″ to .015″ when the rubbing block is on the high point of the cam. Should the breaker points need adjustment, proceed as follows:

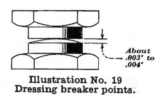

Illustration No. 19
Dressing breaker points.

Inspect the breaker points and if they are pitted, use a sharp magneto point file to polish the contact surfaces. One point should be slightly rounded, about .003″ to .004″ to insure good contact. (*See illustration No. 19.*) Loosen the fixed breaker point lock nut and adjust the fixed breaker point to the thickness of the gauge attached to the magneto wrench marked "Breaker Points." Without changing this adjustment, tighten the fixed breaker point lock nut. When making this adjustment be sure the fiber rubbing block is on the high point of the cam. (*See illustrations Nos. 20 and 21.*)

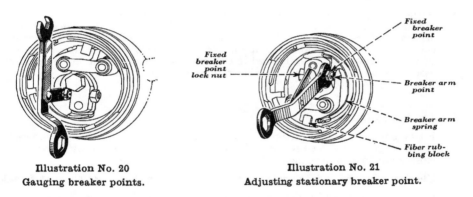

Illustration No. 20
Gauging breaker points.

Illustration No. 21
Adjusting stationary breaker point.

The breaker arm springs should be cleaned and wiped with a piece of cloth dampened with oil at the time the breaker cam is oiled, to prevent the springs from rusting.

The rubbing surface of the cam should always be free from dust and slightly oiled to prevent excessive wear of the fiber rubbing block. (*See illustration No. 16.*)

Distributor

Remove the distributor block after every two to three hundred hours of operation and clean the inside of the block, the face of the distributor disk, and the collector ring on the armature shaft with a cloth moistened with gasoline, and then wipe dry with a clean cloth. The brushes should be inspected to see that they are in good condition and move freely in their guides. (*See illustration No. 16.*) If the brushes are allowed to stick in their guides, they will arc and form a green corrosion on the brass parts. The brush and breaker springs will also be rusted. See that all brushes are free in their guides.

Impulse Coupling

The magneto is equipped with an automatic impulse starter coupling which makes possible the production of a spark, when cranking, equal to the spark when the engine is running.

Failure of the impulse coupling to operate may be caused by heavy oil or dirt and it should be cleaned by flushing it with gasoline while in place on the engine.

If the coupling still fails to operate, the magneto, with coupling attached, should be removed and taken to an authorized service station for repairs.

The coupling cover must always be in place to exclude water and dirt.

At least once a year the magneto, with coupling attached, should be taken to an authorized service station for a general overhauling. In case a service station is not accessible, the coupling should be removed from the magneto by unscrewing the coupling nut. The complete coupling should be washed in gasoline and allowed to dry. It should then be immersed in cream separator or sewing machine oil and re-assembled on the magneto. *(See illustration No. 18.)*

Timing the Magneto

Every engine is correctly timed at the factory and should not be tampered with. If the magneto has been removed for any reason, the following instructions must be closely adhered to in replacing the magneto on the engine.

Check the breaker point opening as outlined under the heading **"Circuit Breaker."**

Secure the magneto in place on the bracket by inserting the magneto base screws loosely in the magneto.

Note: When replacing the magneto base screws, do not use screws longer than the originals as they will damage the armature.

Crank the engine until No. 1 piston (the piston next to the starting crank) is on the upper dead center of the compression stroke. The compression stroke can be determined by removing the No. 1 spark plug and placing the thumb over the opening and cranking the engine until an outward pressure is felt. Continue cranking until the D. C. No. 1 mark on flywheel is in line with timing mark on flywheel housing. Both intake and exhaust valves should be closed at this time.

Timing the Magneto—Continued

Fully retard the spark by raising the breaker housing lever as high as it will go, then carefully remove the breaker housing cover so as to avoid moving the breaker cam.

Remove the distributor block, grasp the magneto half of the adjustment coupling and rotate it clockwise (as viewed from the coupling end) until the segment in the distributor disk is under the distributor block terminal marked "No. 1", and the breaker points are just beginning to open.

The magneto is now correctly timed with the engine. Without changing this setting, replace the magneto coupling shims between the two halves of the adjustment coupling and shift the shims so the cap screws will pass through the holes in the shims and enter the holes in the tapped half of the adjustment coupling.

The coupling is so made that only two of the holes line up exactly opposite to each other and the cap screws must not be forced or the setting will be incorrect.

Replace the distributor block and breaker housing cover, exercising care not to damage the distributor block brushes.

With the spark fully retarded, unhook and slide the impulse coupling cover away from the magneto and crank the engine until the breaker points are just beginning to open, with the impulse coupling disengaged and No. 1 piston coming up on the compression stroke. If the engine is timed correctly, the D. C. No. 1 mark on the flywheel will be in line with the timing mark on the flywheel housing.

The impulse coupling can be disengaged by pressing in the leading end of the top pawl while the engine is being cranked. This prevents this pawl from engaging with the catch plate. (*See illustration No. 17.*)

With the impulse coupling engaged, crank the engine until No. 1 piston is coming up on the compression stroke. Continue to crank the engine slowly, watching to see that mark "**A**" on the coupling member is between the two marks "**B-B**" on the impulse coupling plate when the impulse coupling trips. The impulse coupling cover should then be replaced. (*See illustration No. 18.*)

The D. C. No. 1 mark on the flywheel should be in line with or not more than 8° below ($\frac{25}{32}''$ on flywheel rim), and never above, the timing mark on the flywheel housing when the impulse coupling trips.

Timing the Magneto—Continued

Attach the spark plug cables to the magneto, connecting the No. 1 cable to the terminal on the distributor block marked "**1**". When all cables are connected to the distributor block, slip the magneto cover over the cables and before the cover is fastened in place, connect the cables to the correct spark plugs. Insert the magneto connection through the opening in the magneto cover and fasten the cover in place. (*See illustration No. 22.*)

The magneto is now correctly timed and wired.

Caution! Never operate the engine without the magneto cover in place.

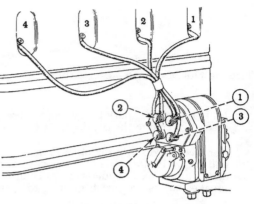

Illustration No. 22—Wiring plan (for E4A Magneto).

☞ Firing order is 1, 3, 4, 2, beginning at radiator end of engine.

Spark Plugs

The spark plug selected after careful tests as best suited for this engine is the Champion No. 1 and should be used unless a good substitute of the same construction can be procured. (*See illustration No. 23.*)

A gap of .020″ to .025″ (or the thickness of the gauge attached to the magneto wrench marked "Spark Plug") should be maintained between the electrodes. When making this adjustment, always bend the outer electrode and never the center electrode as it may damage the insulator. If the gap between the electrodes is too great, due to improper setting or burning off the ends, the spark will jump the safety gap in the magneto, resulting in misfiring. Keep the gaps properly set to the thickness of the gauge.

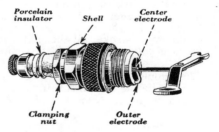

Illustration No. 23

Adjusting spark plug gap.

The spark plugs must be kept clean and for this reason the two-piece construction is used. By removing the clamping nut, the insulator can be removed and thoroughly cleaned by washing it in gasoline or alcohol, and scraping it with a piece of hardwood. The inside of the shell should be scraped clean with a knife while the insulator is out. Be sure that the insulator gasket is in place when re-assembling the plug. (*See illustration No. 23.*)

Caution! Never clean the insulator with anything which will scratch the porcelain as this will damage the glaze, allowing carbon and dirt to accumulate much faster.

WATER SYSTEM

General Information

The cooling of the engine is accomplished by a water circulating pump having a therm static control valve. *The water level must not be allowed to drop below the radiator inlet, otherwise the loss of water will be excessive and the engine will overheat.*

Thermostat

Do not disturb thermostat *(see illustration No. 24)* located in water outlet manifold except when necessary, as it has been adjusted at the factory and requires very little attention. Should radiator show signs of overheating by excessive steaming or motor laboring, *refer to "Corrective Measures" on pages 39 to 41.*

Make sure fan belt is not slipping. The water circulation passages may be blocked or water may fail to circulate through block and cylinder head, due to inoperative thermostat. The engine may fail to warm up properly, due to a leak through ther-

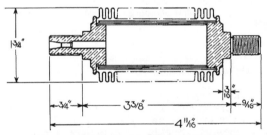

Illustration No. 24—Thermostat (19398DB).

mostat valve seat or because thermostat valves fail to seat. Engine should warm up in from 5 to 8 minutes. When trouble is traced to the thermostat, *refer to instructions for removing thermostat, page 44.*

Examine thermostat valves and valve seats and see that they are seating properly. See that thermostat is free to move in guides. If cause is not found in valves, it is probable that the thermostat has been damaged and must be removed and replaced.

The Radiator

Keep the radiator filled to *3 inches* from top of filler hole, with water which is free from lime, salt, gypsum, sulphur or other impurities. Soft or rain water should be used if same can be readily obtained. Never pour cold water into an empty or nearly empty water system when the engine is very hot. Wait until engine cools off.

When filling radiator, open pet cock on top of water outlet manifold (thermostat cage) and close when water appears. *(See illustration No. 3.)*

To Drain Water System

Open pet cock in water outlet manifold.

Remove drain pipe wing cap located underneath radiator, and open drain cock on side of crankcase to drain cylinder head and crankcase *(See illustration No. 8.)*

Check and see that the water drains through properly.

Leave drains open until ready to fill up cooling system for another run.

The capacity of the water system is about 10 gallons. The water system must be drained when there is danger of freezing, as serious trouble arises if the water freezes in the engine or radiator. *A list showing the properties of anti-freezing solutions may be found on page 37.*

Cleaning the Water System

The radiator and cylinder water jackets should be cleaned occasionally. To clean the radiator, disconnect the connections and flush thoroughly by pouring water in at top and through the radiator onto the ground. The cylinder jackets may be flushed in the same manner. Should the cylinders and radiator become limed up, make a solution of one part muriatic acid and seven parts rain water, and allow this to stand in system for thirty-six hours. Then drain, and flush the entire system with clean water.

For further information on Water System, Fan, etc., see pages 43 and 44.

BEARINGS AND GASKETS

Inspecting and Testing

To determine if the connecting rod bearings are loose, remove the handhole plates on left hand side of engine. Turn engine over until bearing to be tested is nearly at the top dead center of compression stroke. Then place a bar under nut on bearing cap and pry against it; meanwhile place the other hand on bearing and crankshaft and determine by touch what looseness is present.
(See illustration No. 25.)

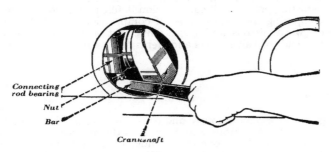

Illustration No. 25
Testing connecting rod bearings for looseness.

If excessive looseness is found, a sufficient amount of shims should be removed to leave about 3/1000″ to 5/1000″ play in the bearings and there should be from 10/1000″ to 15/1000″ side play. The main bearings are ball bearings and do not need adjustment or special attention except *to keep grit away from same;* this is best accomplished by keeping clean oil in crankcase.
(See "Engine Lubrication," page 14.)

Gaskets

Before putting on new gaskets, the surface for the joint must be thoroughly cleaned. When tightening up a joint after a new gasket has been inserted, screw up all nuts fairly snug, then tighten uniformly, giving each nut a small part of a turn at a time, Continue this until all nuts are tight. Do not screw one nut down perfectly tight. and then go to the next, as you will not secure an even pressure on the gasket in this manner. *After engine has been running a few minutes, tighten the nuts again.*

CAUTION—Be sure to adjust valve tappet clearance after the last tightening of cylinder head stud nuts. (See "Valve Adjustment.")

ENGINE

Running a New Engine

Never run a new engine immediately under full load. Work it easily until you are sure that oil has reached all parts. (*See special precautions on page 3.*)

Maintaining Compression

Compression in all cylinders should be equal. Test the compression occasionally by turning the starting crank until compression is felt in each of the four cylinders in succession, comparing the result. Loss of compression is probably due to worn cylinder sleeves, worn pistons and rings, imperfect seating of valves, too little clearance between ends of valve levers and stems or by carbon deposit on the valve seats.

Carbonized Cylinders

In case the engine knocks continuously and does not develop the normal amount of power, it may be that the combustion chamber walls are coated with carbon. If the cylinders are carbonized, remove the cylinder head, scrape off the carbon from the head, piston head and combustion chamber. It is also advisable to regrind the valves at this time.

When replacing cylinder head, follow the instructions *on page 29* under heading "GASKETS" regarding tightening of nuts as it is important to secure an even pressure on all studs.

Grinding Valves

Valves and seats must be kept in good shape. To regrind valves, drain the cooling system, remove the cylinder head, take off the valve springs, then lift out and clean valve and seat with kerosene. Make a paste of fine emery dust and oil, or use a prepared valve grinding compound.

Apply grinding compound to seat of valve. Put the valve in place and revolve it with a screw driver, or better a carpenter's brace with a screw driver bit, turning a few turns to the right and then to the left, lifting the valve off the seat occasionally to let the grinding compound get between the valve and seat. Continue in this manner until the valve and seat show an even surface all the way around. Then wash off with gasoline or kerosene. Be sure there is no dirt or compound left on the valve seat or in parts when assembling. *After grinding valves, it will be found necessary to readjust valve levers to compensate for the wear.*

ENGINE—Continued

Valve Adjustment

The valve levers must be kept properly adjusted, otherwise hard starting and lack of power will result. The firing order of the engine is 1-3-4-2. (*See illustration No. 22*) If, for any reason, the valve setting has been disturbed or cam gear is to be replaced, care must be taken to restore to original setting. To facilitate this, all gears are properly marked and the marked teeth must be meshed together. Every time the nuts are tightened on cylinder head studs, the valve lever must be adjusted by means of the valve lever screws, using the valve clearance gauge *so that there is a clearance of .017" between ends of valve lever and valve stem when valve is closed. This clearance is very necessary.*
(*See illustration No. 26.*)

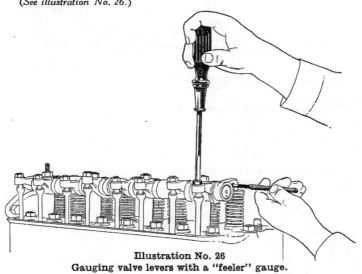

Illustration No. 26
Gauging valve levers with a "feeler" gauge.

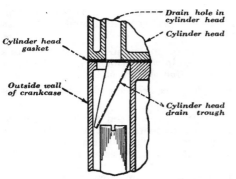

Illustration No. 27
Cylinder head drain trough.

Illustration shows drain trough properly placed to deflect water collected on top of cylinder head from passing into crankcase through breather tube.

CLUTCH

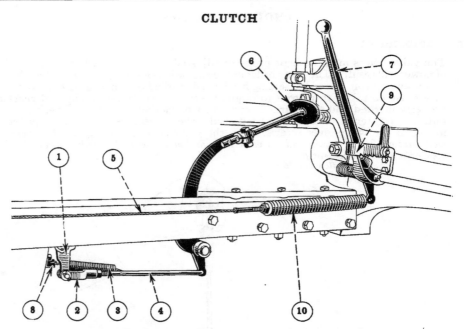

Illustration No. 28—Left side, showing clutch pedal, brake lever, etc.

Ref. No.	DESCRIPTION	Ref. No.	DESCRIPTION
1	Clutch lever.	6	Clutch pedal.
2	Clutch shifter rod fork.	7	Countershaft brake hand lever.
3	Clutch pedal spring.	8	Clutch pedal spring holder.
4	Clutch shifter rod.	9	Countershaft brake hand lever ratchet.
5	Countershaft brake cable.	10	Countershaft brake cable spring.

Care of the Clutch

The clutch is so designed that it requires a minimum of attention. It is important, however, that the clutch release bearing be kept properly lubricated. This can easily be done by following the instructions given below.

About five or six complete strokes of the compressor gun should be applied to this bearing *DAILY, or more often,* if the tractor is used in work which requires frequent clutch operation. *(See illustration No. 67 for location of Zerk fitting.)*

Fill bearing with approved lubricant *(for specifications, see page 13),* using the compressor (supplied with tractor).

It is very important that a clearance be maintained between the clutch release bearing and the clutch release levers. In order to maintain this clearance, the clutch pedal should have a free movement of 1″ to 1⅛″ from the transmission case when the clutch is fully engaged. As the clutch wears, this free movement decreases and adjustment should be made before free movement has become less than ⅞″. Clutch may be badly damaged unless a free movement of foot pedal is maintained. The clutch can easily be reset to the original position by lengthening the rod between foot pedal and clutch shifter lever.

POWER TAKE-OFF

To Operate Power Take-Off with Tractor Running

Throw out the clutch and move power take-off gear shift lever to the right until gears are in mesh, shift transmission gears to the speed that is desired to run the tractor, then slowly let in clutch. (*See illustrations Nos. 2 and 28.*) The power take-off is started and stopped by the same clutch as the tractor. Therefore, be sure to disengage clutch before moving the power take-off gear shift lever.

To Operate Power Take-Off with Tractor Standing Still

The gear shift lever must be in neutral position.

Throw out the clutch and move power take-off gear shift lever to the right until gears are in mesh, then slowly let in clutch. (*See illustrations Nos. 2 and 28.*)

COUNTERSHAFT BRAKE
(*See iilustrations Nos. 2 and 28.*)

The brakes are of the internal expanding type. They are released when the hand lever is in the extreme forward position. To apply the brakes, it is only necessary to pull hand lever back.

BELT PULLEY
(*See illustration on title page*)

The belt pulley is 14⅝ inches in diameter and 7 inches face. The drive is taken from the power take-off shaft through gears to the pulley shaft. These gear shafts and the pulley shaft are mounted on ball bearings.

The gear shift lever must be in neutral position when operating the belt pulley.

Throw out the clutch and push power take-off gear shift lever to the right until gears are in mesh. Then slowly let in clutch. The belt pulley is started and stopped by the same clutch as the tractor. Therefore, be sure to disengage clutch before moving the power take-off gear shift lever.

Steering

(See illustration No. 73.)

The brakes take hold when the front wheels are swung to the extreme right or left, thus causing either of the rear wheels to lock, and the tractor to pivot in its course of travel. The question as to which rear wheel locks depends on the direction of steering; for example, when front wheels are turned to left, the left rear wheel locks and tractor pivots to the left.

Draw Bar and Hitch

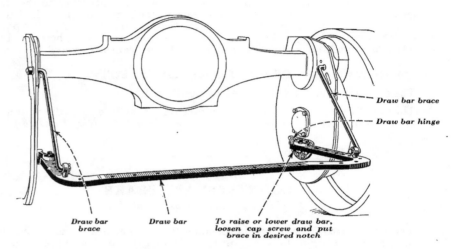

Draw bar brace

Draw bar hinge

Draw bar brace   *Draw bar*   *To raise or lower draw bar, loosen cap screw and put brace in desired notch*

Illustration No. 29—Draw bar.

☞ *Always use the draw bar braces.   Never use chains.*

The tractor exerts its pulling power by means of the draw bar. This is adjusted up and down to accommodate different hitches.   Proper hitching will save both the tractor and the implement it is pulling from undue strains.   The hitch should be made so that the center line of pull of the tractor should fall in line with, or be at least near the center line of draft of the plow or any other hitched-on implement; hitching to one side or the other of the line of draft will cause stresses and strains on both machines, frequently great enough to do permanent injury.   It should be also borne in mind to make the hitch in such a way that the action of the draw bar pull will neither tend to raise the tractor rear wheels from, nor thrust them to the ground as a result of too high or too low hitching.

WARNING!

Do not hitch to the tractor at any point except to the draw bar.

Do not attempt to pull when draw bar is removed.

Always use draw bar and braces.

ADJUSTING RADIATOR CURTAIN

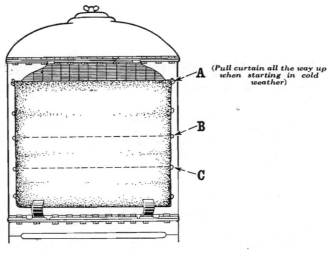

(Pull curtain all the way up when starting in cold weather)

Illustration No. 30

Curtain is supplied with tractor and should be adjusted in warming up as follows:

1.   When starting the engine in freezing weather, set curtain at "A", as shown in illustration, or better still, cover the radiator completely. This will assist in warming up the engine more rapidly and will prevent cold air being drawn through the radiator core and freezing the water in the cooling system.

2.   In cool weather, set curtain at "B".

3.   In non-freezing weather in the early morning or late evening hours, curtain should be adjusted to position "C".

After the engine is thoroughly warmed up the curtain may be lowered completely, except during cold weather. This engine is equipped with water circulating pump having a thermostatic control valve, which circulates the water through the radiator after the engine is warmed up.

Important! Do not start the engine in freezing weather without first covering the radiator *completely*.

Instructions for Care and Operation in Cold Weather

Cold weather offers certain problems to all tractor owners. These are not much of a handicap to the experienced tractor operator, but are likely to be to the man who is wintering his tractor for the first time. In order of their importance these problems are:

1. Danger of water in cylinder jackets freezing with consequent cracking of the cylinders.
2. Faulty lubrication, due to the sluggish action of oils when cold.
3. Difficulty in starting the engine.
4. Storing the tractor for the winter months.

Danger from Freezing

One reason an engine cylinder cracks is because the water around it freezes.

A man may forget to drain his engine or he may not think it is going to be cold enough to freeze the water in the cylinder jackets. No matter how the water happens to be left there, the result is invariably a cracked cylinder, often followed by an extensive outlay for repairs. To avoid anything of this sort, there is one simple precaution to take in cold weather and that is to *drain the water out of the cooling system at the end of every run*. If tractor is to be left standing idle for a few hours, it should be drained.

Where a tractor operator has finished using his tractor, although at that time the weather may not be freezing, he should take care to drain his engine because, when the freezing weather does come, he may have forgotten that he left water in the cooling system.

When engine is left standing for any length of time in freezing weather, crankcase pan should be inspected for water in the oil on account of the possibility of pump freezing and causing breakage.

Draining the Water System

The entire cooling system must be drained during cold weather or when there is danger of freezing. *See special instructions on page 28.*

Adjusting Radiator Curtain

See special instructions on page 35.

Care and Operation in Cold Weather—Continued

Properties of Anti-Freezing Solutions

% By Volume	Denatured Alcohol			Menthanol (Wood Alcohol)			Distilled Glycerine			Ethylene Glycol (Prestone)		
	Freezing Point		Specific Gravity	Freezing Point		Specific Gravity	Freezing Point		Specific Gravity	Freezing Point		Specific Gravity
	°C	°F		°C	°F		°C	°F		°C	°F	
0%	0	32	1.000	0	32	1.000	0	32	1.000	0	32	1.000
10%	−3	27	.988	−5	23	.987	−2	29	1.029	−3	26	1 016
20%	−7	19	.978	−12	10	.975	−6	21	1.057	−9	16	1.031
30%	−12	10	.968	−19	−2	.963	−11	12	1 085	−16	3	1.045
40%	−19	−2	.957	−29	−20	.952	−18	0	1.112	−24	−11	1.058
50%	−28	−18	.943	−40	−40	.937	−26	−15	1 140	−35	−31	1.070

Do not use a solution of Calcium Chloride or any Alkaline solution—they are injurious to the metal parts.

Danger from Thick Transmission Lubricant

In cold weather transmission lubricant of other than approved specifications often becomes thick and heavy and *care should be taken to see that it is diluted sufficiently with a lighter oil so that it will flow readily*, otherwise it will channel and stick to the sides of the case and not flow back to the bottom of the case from where the gears can carry it over the bearings and gears.

Failure of the transmission lubricant to flow readily will soon cause the bearings to be without lubrication.

Overloading

Never overload the tractor; to do best work the machine should only have a normal load under normal speed. Overloading a tractor means ruining it. In running a tractor the operator soon recognizes the sound and regularity of the exhaust as an indication of its speed and running condition. An overload reduces the normal speed of the engine which in turn cuts down the number of exhaust sounds per minute. Any load which slows the tractor down in this manner is an overload and is more than the prescribed amount it should pull with safety.

CARE OF TRACTOR IN STORING AND HOUSING

When a tractor is not to be used for a period of time, it should be stored in a dry and protected place. To leave a tractor stand in an open field or yard exposed to rain and snow, will result in materially shortening the life of the tractor. And, since surely nobody would leave an automobile or auto truck days and nights in the open air, but run it at least under a shed, the same care must be taken also with the tractor.

Special Notice

Always mention number of tractor when ordering repairs.

Number is stamped on name plate on tool box.

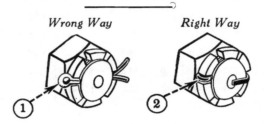

Wrong Way   *Right Way*

Illustration No. 31

Wrong and Right Way to secure a Cotter Pin

1. Head of cotter not in slot of nut—turned wrong. Ends not split right—turned wrong. This combination will soon work loose and come out.

2. Head of cotter in right—pound down firm—a snug fit in hole. End of cotter pounded back over end of bolt—other end pounded down. Cotter should be tight.

For Cultivating

Less effort will be required if the operator will follow the method outlined *in illustration No. 32*, passing two or more rows at the ends.

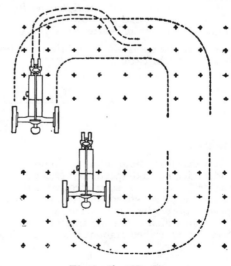

Illustration No. 32

CORRECTIVE MEASURES

Study the problem before making any changes.

If any adjustments are to be disturbed, the original setting should be noted, so this same setting may be restored in case the part changed does not remedy the trouble.

Failure to Start:

No fuel.
Fuel strainer needle valve closed.
Carburetor choked too much.
Magneto grounded.
Throttle control lever improperly set.
Gears engaged.
Kerosene instead of gasoline in fuel strainer (for starting).

Also see **"Missing and Backfiring."**

Missing and Backfiring:

Water in the fuel.
Air leaks around the intake manifold.
Engine not warmed up.
Red-hot carbon deposits in cylinder.

Also see **"Lack of Compression," "Excess Fuel," "Lack of Fuel," "Defective Ignition."**

Irregular Speed:

Governor sticking, out of adjustment, or worn.
Throttle shaft bent or out of alignment.

Also see **"Missing and Backfiring."**

Lack of Oil Pressure:

Insufficient amount of oil.
Oil diluted or not as specified.
Oil filter clogged.
Dirt under the oil pressure regulating valve.
Broken oil gauge.
Oil pump strainer clogged or pump not working.

CORRECTIVE MEASURES—Continued

Lack of Power:

Governor out of adjustment.
Exhaust pipe clogged.
Throttle control lever improperly set.
Clutch slipping.

Also see **"Missing and Backfiring," "Lack of Compression," "Overheating," "Lack of Fuel," "Defective Ignition," "Excess Fuel."**

Knocking:

Spark too far advanced.
Excess carbon in the cylinders.
Sticky valve or improperly adjusted valves.
Loose piston pin, connecting rod, camshaft, or crankshaft bearings.
Broken piston rings or loose pistons.

Also see **"Overheating."**

Lack of Compression:

Sticky, dirty, pitted or improperly adjusted valves.
Stuck, worn or broken piston rings.
Worn pistons.
Leaky cylinder head gasket.

Also see **"Lack of Oil Pressure."**

Overheating:

Spark retarded.
Insufficient amount of water.
Fan belt slipping.
Excess load.
Inside of radiator and cylinder block limed up or clogged with dirt
Outside of radiator or radiator screen covered with dirt or chaff.
Excess carbon in the cylinders.
Carburetor improperly adjusted.

Also see **"Lack of Oil Pressure," "Excess Fuel," "Defective Ignition."**

CORRECTIVE MEASURES—Continued

Excess Fuel Consumption:

Choke out.
Spark retarded too far.
Air pipe screen or air filter clogged.
Incorrect amount or improper grade of oil.
Leaky carburetor fuel valve.

Also see **"Lack of Compression," "Defective Ignition."**

Lack of Fuel:

Fuel low in the tank.
Vent hole in fuel tank filler cap plugged.
Fuel strainer needle valve closed or only partially opened.
Clogged fuel strainer screen, fuel line or carburetor strainer.
Idling adjusting screw not properly set.

Defective Ignition:

Wrong kind, old, cracked, dirty or poorly set spark plugs.
Broken, loose or improperly connected wiring.
Dirty distributor block disk or collector ring.
Stuck or broken brushes.
Dirty, pitted or improperly set breaker points.
Breaker arm not free on its bearing or the breaker arm spring weak or broken.
Ground contact, ground contact spring insulation or spring defective.
Magneto not timed correctly with the engine.
Impulse coupling dirty, dry or lubricated with heavy oil.

If the above items have been corrected and the magneto still fails to function, it should be taken to the nearest authorized service station for overhauling.

Explosions in exhaust pipe often occur just after starting, due to first charges not firing in cylinder and passing through into exhaust pipe, where burning gases from first few explosions will ignite them.

ILLUSTRATIONS AND INSTRUCTIONS
FOR "OVERHAULING"

This section contains instructions and illustrations pertaining to certain simple adjustments and replacements which can readily be made. However, the owner should consult the dealer before attempting a general overhauling or when any mechanical difficulties occur, as he has the necessary equipment for doing the work.

INDEX—"OVERHAULING"

WATER COOLING SYSTEM

Fan and Fan Belt

The fan is driven from the crankshaft by an endless belt. If radiator gives signs of overheating by excessive steaming or the engine laboring, examine the belt for slippage. Due to atmospheric conditions or prolonged use, the fan belt becomes loose; for adjustment, release the set screw in flange on upper pulley and rotate the flange until the belt tension is sufficient to overcome slippage. Tighten set screw in notch provided in hub and tighten lock nut. (*See illustration No. 8.*)

Removing Fan Belt

Drain the water cooling system; remove air intake pipe between oil air filter and carburetor; remove the radiator outlet elbow. Loosen the bolts and remove the starting crank bracket, which will loosen the starting crank.

Loosen the fan housing by removing the four cap screws.

Now loosen the set screw in outer flange on upper pulley and unscrew flange as far as possible toward blades. Start belt over bottom pulley and pry out with a light bar or rod (*see illustration No. 33*), at the same time turning over fan, when belt will work off of pulley. The belt can then be slipped over the top pulley and over the fan blades.

It is recommended that the radiator be removed or at least loosened sufficiently to allow clearance between the fan blades and radiator core for removing the fan belt.

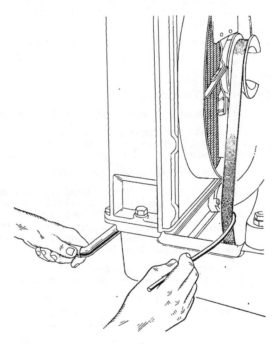

Illustration No. 33

Replacing Fan Belt

In replacing the belt the reverse procedure should be followed, except that belt can be started on lower pulley by hand and by slowly turning engine over, belt will find correct position. Adjust fan belt to avoid slippage, as outlined in paragraph under **"Fan and Fan Belt."**

Water Pump
(See illustration No. 8.)

Due to wear after considerable service, the pump may leak. When this occurs, use a spanner wrench and tighten up on packing gland.

To replace packing, remove water pump, complete, and disassemble. It is recommended that the radiator be removed to gain free access to the pump.

To remove the pump, release set screws in outer flange of fan pulley and unscrew flange to relieve tension on belt. Loosen hose connections to the pump. The pump is attached to cylinder head with screws; remove the screws and the entire assembly can be lifted out.

To reassemble, reverse the above procedure.

To Remove Thermostat

Drain water system to level of flange on water outlet manifold.

Disconnect and remove elbow and hose connections from thermostat cage to upper water tank, remove thermostat cage, complete, by releasing four cap screws through thermostat cage and water outlet manifold.

Remove the thermostat cage carefully so as not to injure the thermostat.

Examine the thermostat connections and see that they are tight. The thermostat valve, when properly adjusted, is held up on its seat with sufficient tension to make it difficult to turn by hand. Should valve turn easily, remove the thermostat from cage, hold at both ends and try to stretch it by hand; when thermostat is in good condition, it will be difficult to stretch; when thermostat stretches easily, replace by new. *(See illustration No. 51.)*

The engine can be operated with thermostat and thermostat valve removed if absolutely necessary, but this is not recommended.

In this case, the cage may be assembled without thermostat and valves, and engine operated, but the passage from the pump to the manifold must be blocked off with a thin metal gasket, with vellumoid gaskets on both sides, or engine will overheat.

To Adjust Bellows
(See illustration No. 51.)

1. Hold valve "A" on valve seat by hand and adjust nut "B" to hold valve in place without stretching bellows.

2. Turn nut "B" one turn to the right and lock in position with jam nut "C".

FRONT WHEELS

Adjusting Front Wheel Bearing

To adjust front wheel bearing, run the opposite wheel on a block of wood as shown *in illustration No. 34.* Remove the three cap screws and take off the hub cap. Straighten the nut lock "**C**" and remove the nut "**D**"; take off the adjusting lock "**A**," and turn the adjusting nut "**B**" to the right until just snug, at the same time rotating the wheel several turns. Then turn the nut "**B**," back about one-sixteenth of a turn and re-assemble by placing adjusting lock "**A**" so one of the holes fits over pin in the adjusting nut "**B**." Replace nut lock "**C**," locating the small projection on side opposite pin in nut "**B**." Replace the nut "**D**," bend the nut lock, and replace hub cap and the three cap screws.

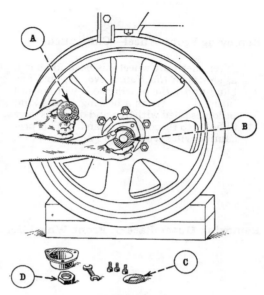

Illustration No. 34

Removing Front Wheel

To remove the front wheel, proceed as shown *in illustration No. 34,* and in addition take off the adjusting nut. Oftentimes the wheel can be "rocked off." If this fails, use a stick of wood as shown *in illustration No. 35* and gently tap the wheel until it is loosened. (*Also see illustration No. 36.*)

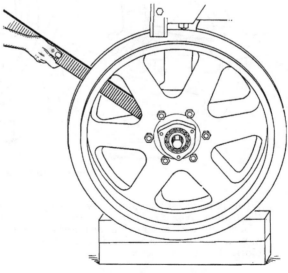

Illustration No. 35

Removing Front Wheel—Continued

After the front wheel has been loosened, as shown *in illustration No. 35*, hold one hand under the bearing so it will not fall in the dirt. When a bearing of this kind becomes filled with dirt and dust it is very difficult to thoroughly clean it. This precaution will save time and difficulty later.

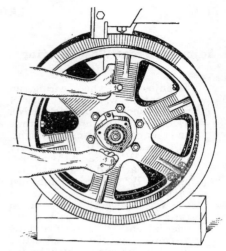

Illustration No. 36

Removing Outer Race of Front Wheel Bearing

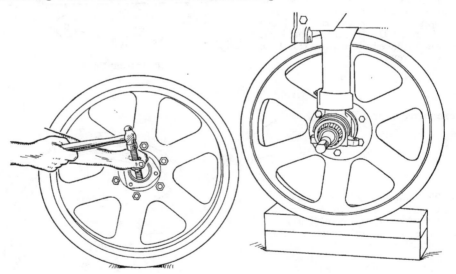

Illustration No. 37

When it is necessary to put new bearings in the front wheel, proceed as shown *in illustrations Nos. 34, 35 and 36*. In removing, set the wheel as shown *in illustration No. 37* and with a bar drive the outer race out of place. When the new race is to be put in, be very careful that it is started in straight and tap it in place by using a block of wood laid across it.

Removing Front Wheel Inner Bearing and Race

After removing the wheel, the inner roller bearing and its inner race will remain on the spindle. These can be removed by prying off with a screw driver if no better tool is available. (*See illustration No. 38*.) If the felt washer is injured in this procedure, re-replace with a new one.

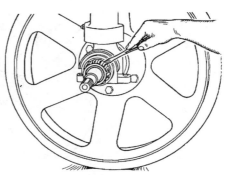

Illustration No. 38

Replacing Front Wheel Bearing

In replacing the front wheel and bearing, care should be exercised not to injure the bearing. Put the wheel on and see that the felt washers on the inside of the wheel are not sheared off or injured. Place the outer bearing on the end of the shaft and with a clean block of wood gently tap it into the proper position. (*See illustration No. 39.*)

Proceed from this point as described *on page 45*, which will give the proper adjustment to the bearing.

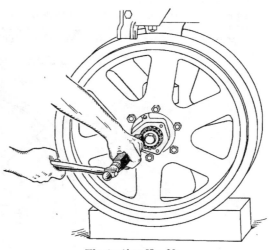

Illustration No. 39

REAR WHEELS

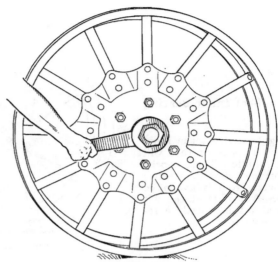

Illustration No. 40

Removing Rear Wheel

In removing the rear wheel, first block up the drive gear housing as shown *in illustration No. 41*. Straighten the rear axle nut lock washer and remove the check nut and rear axle nut. *(See illustration No. 40.)* The wheel may now be easily removed.

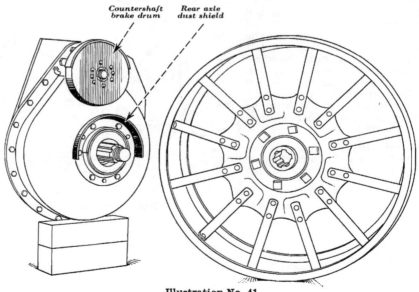

Countershaft brake drum   Rear axle dust shield

Illustration No. 41

REAR AXLE, TRANSMISSION, BELT PULLEY

Care of Rear Axle Oil Seal Diaphragm

(See illustration No. 74.)

In rice field service or when tractor is operated under other extremely muddy conditions, the rear axle oil seal diaphragm and pressure plate assembly **(12)** should be taken out about once a season and any dirt that has collected between it and the oil seal guard **(8)** should be removed. At this time the diaphragm should also be soaked in oil.

To remove the above assembly, proceed as follows:

Remove the rear wheel *(see page 48)*, take out the cap screws holding the outer bearing **(10)** and oil seal diaphragm assembly to countershaft housing and remove retainer and seal.

To reassemble, reverse the above procedure, taking care that pressure plate springs are properly set in place and that outer bearing retainer is assembled with centering pin at top. Replace retainer gasket **(7)** if necessary.

☞*For reference numbers mentioned above, see illustration No. 74.*

Replacing Transmission Shaft Packing

To remove the transmission shaft packing, take out the five cap screws which hold the dust shield over the transmission joint. Then loosen the cap screw holding the packing gland lock. Using the spanner wrench found in the tool box, turn the packing gland as far out as possible. Remove the old packing with a large nail or hooked wire and insert new packing as shown *in illustration No. 42.*

Note: It is not necessary to remove any parts other than those mentioned.

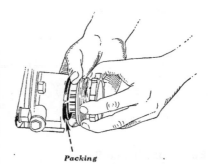

Packing

Illustration No. 42

Replacing Belt Pulley Shaft Packing

To remove the pulley shaft packing, loosen cap screw holding the packing gland lock and turn the packing gland out as far as possible with the spanner wrench found in the tool box. Remove the old packing with a large nail or hooked wire and insert new packing as shown *in illustration No. 43.*

Note: It is not necessary to remove belt pulley.

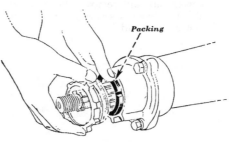

Packing

Illustration No. 43

COUNTERSHAFT BRAKE

Brake Cable Adjustment

The brakes are adjusted by means of an eye-bolt attached to the steel steering cables. The front wheels must be in line with the center line of the tractor, the cables just taut and of such length that the brake operating levers lay back against the countershaft housing, which is the released position of the brake cam. At this point there must be no tension on the springs.

Removing the Brake Drum

First take off the large nut which holds the brake drum in place. Straighten up and remove lockwasher and pry off the brake drum. It may be necessary to use a puller to remove the drum.

Adjusting Brake for Wear

Some operators make the mistake of resting a foot on the brake lever which causes undue wear of the brake lining; this may also spring the brake shaft. If one finds that the brake doesn't take hold and yet doesn't show that it is worn out, it can be fixed as shown *in illustration No. 44*. Remove the wearing plate, "A," and place some shims, "B," under it. This will give the brake more braking contact. When relining brakes, the shims, "B," must be removed because the new lining is thicker.

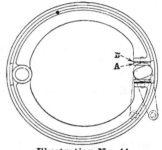

Illustration No. 44

Brake drum removed

Brake band and lining

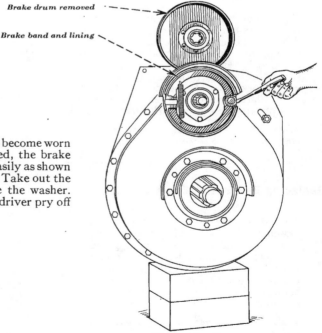

Removing Brake Band

Should the brake lining become worn and need to be replaced, the brake band can be removed easily as shown *in illustration No. 45*. Take out the cotter pin and remove the washer. With a chisel or screw driver pry off the brake band.

Illustration No. 45

List and Illustrations

Detailed illustrations of the principal units are included in this section, together with list showing the numbers and description of parts.

INDEX

ILLUSTRATIONS AND LIST

COMPLETE TRACTOR

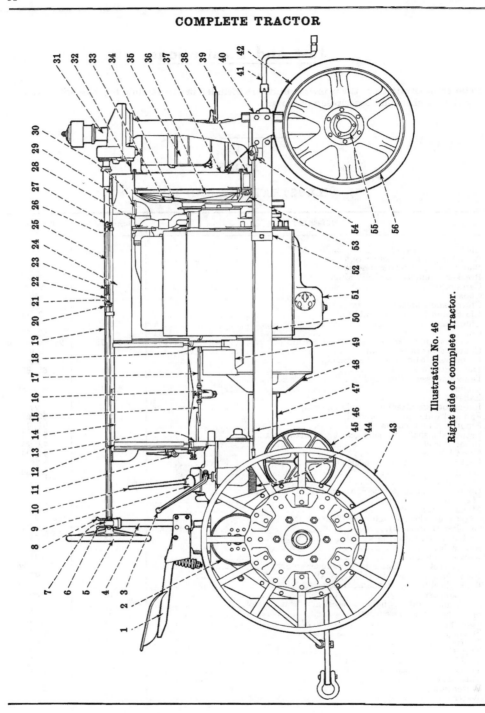

Illustration No. 46
Right side of complete Tractor.

COMPLETE TRACTOR

(See illustration No. 46)

Ref. No.	I H C Part No.	DESCRIPTION
1	19877D	Seat support (3", 5-lb. channel).
2	2248DX	Countershaft brake drum, complete.
3	2333D	Power take-off shifter hand lever.
4	19878D	Steering shaft bearing post.
5	1526D	Steering wheel.
6	1438D	Throttle rod hand lever.
7	1598DX	Steering shaft bearing.
8	1439D	Spark rod hand lever.
9	1518DCX	Gear shift ball socket cap.
10	15047DA	Gear shifter lever.
11	2317D	Heat control hand lever.
12	19871D	Fuel tank strap.
13	2282D	Fuel tank bracket, rear.
14	19872DX	Fuel tank, complete with caps.
15	19885DX	Fuel pipe to gasoline tank, complete.
16	17237D	Fuel tank strainer.
17	20602DX	Fuel pipe to carburetor, complete.
18	2281D	Fuel tank bracket, front.
19	19882D	Steering shaft.
20	431EB	Spark rod lever.
21	19783D	Spark tube connection.
22	19883D	Spark tube.
23	10862D	Throttle rod spring.
24	19879DX	Hood sheet, complete.
25	19884D	Throttle rod.
26	19848D	Throttle rod connection.
27	2431D	Throttle rod lever.
28	19840D	Radiator inlet elbow hose.
29	2277DX	Water tank, upper, complete.
30	2273D	Radiator inlet elbow.
31	15736DY	Air pipe, complete with strainer.
32	2283D	Oil air filter top (7" diam.).
33	11337D	Carburetor connection hose.
34	20601D	Carburetor connection.
35	19111DX	Oil air filter, complete.
36	19874D	Fan housing sheet.
37	2275D	Radiator core spacer, L. H.
37	2276D	Radiator core spacer, R. H.
38	2348DAX	Water tank, lower, complete.
39	15107D	Cultivator shifter lever.
40	2328DX	Cultivator pivot bracket, L. H., complete.
40	2329DX	Cultivator pivot bracket, R. H., complete.
41	15179DAX	Starting crank, complete.
42	15360DB	Front wheel tire ring.
43	20175DA	Rear wheel, complete, less lugs (12").
44	19836D	Brake cable spring.
45	2272D	Belt pulley (14⅝" diam. x 7" face).
46	19832DX	Countershaft brake cable.
47	19926D	Clutch joint shield.
48	2316D	Clutch housing.
49	19865D	Tool box.
50	19864D	Main frame.
51	14762D	Crankcase pan, complete with oil trough.
52	15352D	Brake cable guide.
53	2349D	Radiator outlet elbow.
54	1551DA	Countershaft brake sheave.
55	12312D	Front wheel hub cap.
56	2240D	Front wheel.

ENGINE (Right Side)

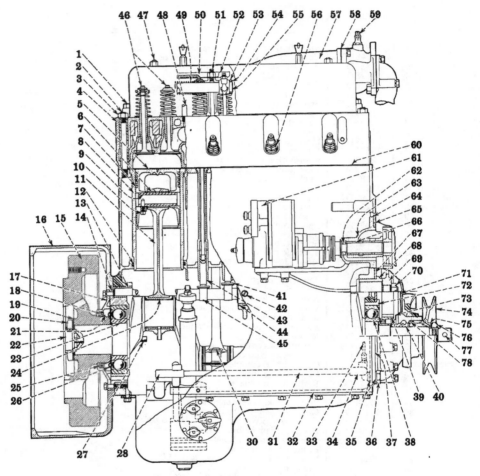

Illustration No. 47

Engine (4¼ x 5″), right side

(sectional view).

ENGINE (Right Side)

(See illustration No. 47.)

Ref. No.	I H C Part No.	DESCRIPTION	Ref. No.	I H C Part No.	DESCRIPTION
1	10408D	Water outlet manifold stud, short ($\frac{1}{2}$ x 7$\frac{1}{16}$").	36	10493DA	Oil discharge elbow nut.
2	8000T	Cylinder head stud, short ($\frac{1}{2}$ x 6$\frac{3}{8}$").	37	10420D	Crankcase front plate gasket.
			38	10399D	Main bearing, front.
3	4097DA	Cylinder head stud nut.	39	10383D	Crankshaft pinion (28 teeth).
4	2291DAX	Cylinder head, complete.	40	10320D	Crankshaft pinion spacer.
	2291DAY	Cylinder head, complete with valves.	41	10332D	Valve tappet.
5	2366DX	Piston, complete less rings.	42	7115T	Camshaft rear bearing lock screw.
	2366DY	Piston, complete with rings.	43	431D	Valve tappet guide.
6	7176TA	Connecting rod bushing.	44	10310DB	Camshaft center bearing.
7	20279D	Piston ring (oil control).	45	19904D	Camshaft.
	20273D	Piston ring (compression).	46	....	Valve assembly.
8	435DX	Cylinder sleeve with packing ring.	47	17618D	Valve lever pin stud, long.
			48	10322DA	Cylinder priming tube.
9	7144TA	Piston pin.	49	12209D	Valve lever spring.
10	4787T	Piston pin set screw ($\frac{1}{2}$ x 1$\frac{1}{2}$").	50	4042D	Valve lever oil trough packing.
11	10393DBX	Connecting rod, complete.	51	4039D	Valve lever pin stud, short.
12	822C	Cylinder sleeve packing ring (rubber).	52	4043D	Valve lever oil trough.
			53	12231D	Valve lever collar pin ($\frac{5}{32}$ x 1$\frac{1}{2}$").
13	16738DA	Camshaft bearing, rear.	54	12208D	Valve lever pin collar.
14	442D	Main bearing retainer, rear.	55	8014TA	Valve lever pin (1 x 9$\frac{5}{8}$").
15	2292D	Flywheel.	56	13117D	Spark plug (Champion No. 1).
16	2293DX	Bell housing, complete.	57	2301D	Water outlet manifold.
17	441DA	Main bearing cover plate.	58	18728D	Thermostat cage gasket.
18	12748D	Crankshaft felt washer, rear.	59	17602D	Thermostat cage air vent drain cock.
19	10354D	Flywheel nut lock.	60	19905D	Cylinder head gasket.
20	10353D	Flywheel nut (2$\frac{1}{4}$").	61	E4A-347-A	Magneto, complete.
21	12749D	Crankshaft felt washer retainer.	62	16373D	Magneto drive shaft oil flinger.
22	10379DAX	Crankshaft, complete with wick.	63	1906DAX	Magneto bracket, complete.
23	10400D	Main bearing, rear.	64	10367D	Magneto bracket gasket.
24	10909DBX	Connecting rod bearing, complete (2 halves, undersize, .020").	65	10419D	Crankcase front cover gasket.
			66	16552D	Magneto drive shaft bushing.
			67	10382DA	Crankcase front plate.
25	12750D	Main bearing cover plate washer.	68	10311DB	Camshaft front bearing.
26	10355D	Main bearing oil deflector.	69	10384DX	Camshaft gear, complete.
27	12219D	Clutch shaft bearing wick.	70	4221D	Camshaft nut ($\frac{1}{2}$ x 1$\frac{7}{16}$").
28	1496D	Oil discharge bracket.	71	497DAX	Crankcase front cover with plug.
29	....		72	436D	Main bearing retainer, front.
30	8047TAX	Connecting rod bolt, complete.	73	10317D	Crankshaft pinion washer.
31	14855D	Oil discharge pipe, complete.	74	2300D	Fan drive pulley.
32	10421D	Crankcase pan gasket.	75	10374D	Crankshaft pinion nut lock.
33	10411D	Camshaft gear oil pipe.	76	10316D	Crankshaft pinion nut ($\frac{1}{2}$x2$\frac{1}{8}$").
34	14848D	Oil discharge elbow.	77	10319D	Starting crank pin.
35	4301D	Oil discharge elbow gasket.	78	12734D	Crankshaft felt washer, front.

ENGINE (Front View)

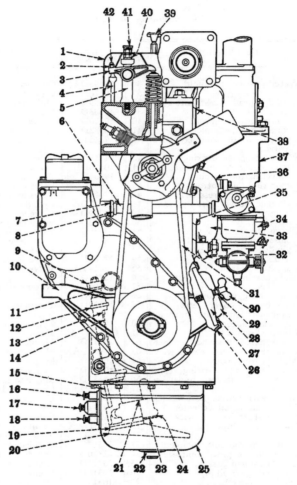

Illustration No. 48

Engine (4¼ x 5″), front view (sectional).

ENGINE (Front View)

(See illustration No. 48.)

Ref. No.	I H C Part No.	DESCRIPTION
1	19903DX	Valve housing, complete.
2	10952D	Valve lever screw check nut.
3	19898DX	Valve lever and bushing, complete.
4	10365D	Valve push rod.
5	7974TB	Valve lever pin support.
6	12744D	Governor connecting rod housing.
7	12720D	Governor connecting rod housing felt washer retainer.
8	12726D	Governor connecting rod housing felt washer.
9	10335D	Oil pump drive pinion (10 teeth).
10	10644D	Motor support, front.
11	445D	Oil pump shaft bushing.
12	406DBXa	Oil pump body, complete with bushing and pin.
13	10337D	Oil pump shaft collar.
14	10368D	Oil pump shaft.
15	14413D	Oil discharge pipe (vertical).
16	1998T	Oil gauge cock (¾").
17	1994TA	Crankcase oil drain valve (1").
18	1998T	Oil gauge cock (¾").
19	413D	Oil pump cover.
20	10346D	Oil pump screen holder, complete.
21	15840D	Oil pressure valve body gasket.
22	7061T	Crankcase pan drain flange.
23	14415D	Oil pressure valve cover.
24	14416D	Oil pressure valve gasket.
25	14762D	Crankcase pan, complete with oil trough.
26	437DCXb	Crankcase, complete.
27	4083D	Handhole cover clamp.
28	4080D	Handhole cover.
29	4112D	Handhole cover clamp bolt gasket.
30	7167T	Handhole cover clamp bolt.
31	18764D	Fan belt.
32	19337D	Crankcase drain plug.
33	2299D	Crankcase inlet elbow.
34	20590D	Carburetor, complete (Zenith Model K-5).
35	12235D	Water inlet elbow gasket.
36	2321DX	Water pump outlet pipe, complete.
37	2302DX	Intake manifold, complete.
38	10413DA	Exhaust and intake manifold gasket.
39	13106D	Cylinder head priming cup.
40	4319D	Valve lever pin stud spacer.
41	13143D	Valve lever oiler.
42	10951D	Valve lever screw.

ENGINE

Miscellaneous parts not indicated in illustrations Nos. 47 and 48.

I H C Part No.	DESCRIPTION
2323D	Thermostat cage flange.
4095D	Piston pin (oversize .005").
4299D	Oil pump impeller gear pin ($\frac{9}{16}$ x $1\frac{1}{2}$").
10336D	Pump impeller gear, driven (12 teeth).
10344D	Pump impeller gear, driver (12 teeth).
10410D	Flywheel key.
10422D	Water outlet manifold gasket.
10434D	Crankcase pan oil level flange.
10497D	Main bearing cover plate gasket.
10499D	Crankcase breather pipe.
10630D	Radiator gasket plate, rear.
10944D	Camshaft gear shim.
10954DA	Cylinder head drain trough.
11252D	Camshaft gear shim.
12257D	Piston pin (oversize .010").
12258D	Piston pin (oversize .015").
12261D	Cylinder sleeve shim.
12298DA	Connecting rod bearing shim.
12733DBX	Connecting rod bearing, complete (2 halves, undersize $\frac{1}{32}$")
12769D	Connecting rod and cap, complete.
13055D	Crankshaft pinion key.
13055D	Fan drive pulley key.
13061D	Camshaft gear oil pipe connector.
13072D	Camshaft bearing bore (cork).
15841D	Oil pressure valve with body and spring.
15841DX	Oil pressure valve, complete.
15950D	Oil pump gasket.
16206D	Oil pump, complete.
16734DX	Crankshaft, complete (undersize $\frac{1}{32}$").
16739D	Crankcase gasket, rear.
17168D	Manifold heat control valve key.
17171DX	Crankshaft (undersize $\frac{1}{32}$").
17562D	Crankcase front cover expansion plug (1").
18743D	Water outlet manifold stud (2nd intermediate, $\frac{1}{2}$ x $9\frac{3}{16}$").
18744D	Water manifold stud (intermediate, $\frac{1}{2}$ x 9").
18745D	Water outlet manifold stud, long ($\frac{1}{2}$ x $10\frac{11}{16}$").
18800D	Thermostat cage outlet pipe hose.
18800D	Crankcase inlet elbow hose.
19953D	Fan housing cap gasket.
19982D	Thermostat cage flange gasket.
20073D	Cylinder sleeve with piston, complete.
20074D	Cylinder sleeve with piston and cylinder head gasket.
20152D	Gasket (package for repairs).
20312D	Cylinder head intake venturi.
20324D	Exhaust and intake manifold washer.
20328D	Speed change lever pin.
20329D	Speed change shaft packing.
20505D	Fan drive pulley mud shield (special).
G 3102	Crankcase breather nipple (street ell).
G 3243	Water inlet elbow stud ($\frac{7}{16}$ x $1\frac{5}{8}$").
G 6193	Crankcase breather pipe.
3405H	Spark plug gasket.
1671TC	Connecting rod shims (package).
4167T	Oil pump shaft key.
6220T	Oil pump shaft bushing pin.
7102$\frac{1}{2}$T	Handhole cover gasket.
7115T	Camshaft center bearing lock screw.
7198TA No. 1	Water pump outlet pipe gasket.
7220T	Camshaft gear key.
7991T	Valve lever bushing.
8029T	Oil pump shaft collar pin.
8298TCX	Connecting rod bearing.
8349T	Connecting rod bolt nut.

VALVE ASSEMBLY

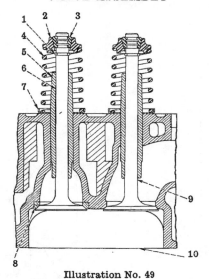

Illustration No. 49

Valve assembly (sectional view).

Ref. No.	IHC Part No.	DESCRIPTION
1	18539D	Valve stem retainer.
2	19902D	Valve spring seat, upper.
3	20312H	Valve spring seat key.
4	19899D	Valve spring.
5	2290D	Valve stem guide..
6	19900D	Exhaust valve.
7	18746D	Valve spring seat, lower.
8	2361DA	Valve seat insert.
9	19901D	Intake valve.
10	2291DAX	Cylinder head.
	2291DAY	Cylinder head, complete with valves.

SPARK AND THROTTLE, CHOKE, EXHAUST AND HEAT CONTROL

IHC Part No.	DESCRIPTION
2286D	Heat control lever bracket.
11901D	Heat control hand lever spring.
14038DA	Choke rod clip.
19305D	Heat control rod end.
19306D	Head control rod end pin.
19867D	Heat control rod.
19870D	Choke rod, front.
19931D	Heat control hand lever pivot.
19962D	Exhaust pipe stud nut.
20246D	Exhaust pipe gasket.
3843T	Heat control hand lever pin.
9663T	Throttle rod hand lever pin.

FAN AND WATER PUMP ASSEMBLY

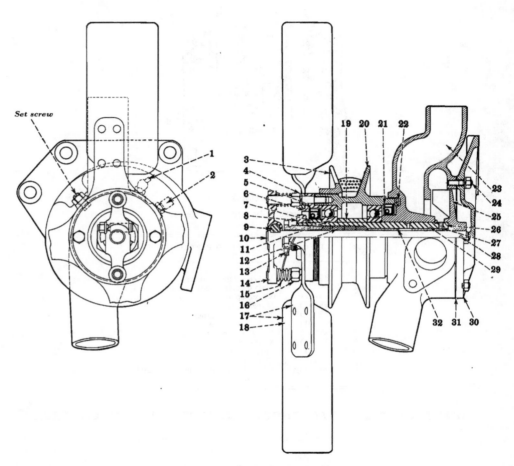

Illustration No. 50
Fan and water pump assembly (sectional view).

FAN AND WATER PUMP ASSEMBLY

(See illustration No. 50.)

Ref. No.	I H C Part No.	DESCRIPTION
1	14187D	Fan hub bearing lubricator ($\frac{1}{8}$") (Zerk).
2	19175D	Water pump lubricator ($\frac{1}{8}$") with cap (Zerk).
3	2370D	Fan and water pump pulley flange.
4	. . . .	Lock washer ($\frac{5}{16}$ x $\frac{1}{16}$").
5	20289D	Water pump oil seal, front.
6	20306DX	Water pump bearing retainer, complete.
7	20293D	Water pump bearing lock sleeve.
8	.20299D	Water pump bearing clamp nut.
9	20586D	Water pump driver pin.
10	20584D	Water pump shaft.
11	20308D	Water pump ball bearing.
12	20302DA	Water pump shaft packing.
13	20296D	Water pump packing gland.
14	20585D	Water pump driver.
15	G 3792	Water pump driver spring.
16	20301D	Water pump driver stud.
17	20510D	Fan blade carrier with blades.
18	20374D	Fan blade.
19	20297D	Water pump bearing spacer.
20	2369DX	Fan and water pump pulley hub, complete.
21	20290D	Water pump oil seal, rear.
22	20300D	Water pump felt washer.
23	2371DX	Water pump body assembly.
24	11657D	Water pump body stud.
25	2368DA	Water pump impeller.
26	20298DA	Water pump impeller thrust washer.
27	20303D	Water pump thrust bushing.
28	20288D	Water pump impeller pin.
29	20305DX	Water pump shaft sleeve assembly.
30	2372D	Water pump cover.
31	19915D	Water pump cover gasket.
32	20304D	Water pump shaft bushing.

THERMOSTAT ASSEMBLY

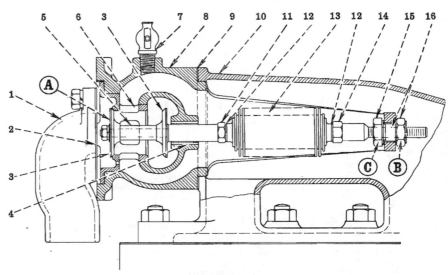

Illustration No. 51

Thermostat assembly (sectional view).

Ref. No.	IHC Part No.	DESCRIPTION
1	2322D	Thermostat cage outlet pipe.
2	7198TA No. 1	Thermostat cage outlet pipe gasket.
3	19917D	Thermostat valve.
4	19584D	Thermostat valve shaft bushing.
5	19918DA	Thermostat valve spacer.
6	2224D	Thermostat valve seat.
7	17602D	Thermostat cage air vent drain cock.
8	2297DX	Thermostat valve cage, complete.
9	18728D	Thermostat cage gasket.
10	2301D	Water outlet manifold.
11	19916D	Thermostat valve shaft.
12	19588D	Thermostat lockwasher ($\frac{7}{16}$"—"Shakeproof").
13	19398DB	Water control thermostat.
14	19585D	Thermostat adapter shaft.
15	19587D	Thermostat adapter shaft nut.
16	19586D	Thermostat adapter shaft bushing (nut).

To Adjust Bellows:

1.   Hold valve "A" on valve seat by hand and adjust nut "B" to hold valve in place without stretching bellows.

2.   Turn nut "B" one turn to the right and lock in position with jam nut "C."

RADIATOR

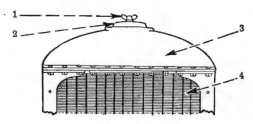

Illustration No. 52

Ref. No.	IHC Part No.	DESCRIPTION
1	7167T	Water tank handhole cover clamp bolt.
2	4080D	Water tank handhole cover with clamp stop.
3	2277DX	Water tank, upper (mention "name" of tractor when ordering).
4	19841D	Radiator core, complete.

RADIATOR AND WATER TANK

Miscellaneous parts not indicated in illustration No. 52.

IHC Part No.	DESCRIPTION	IHC Part No.	DESCRIPTION
4083D	Water tank handhole cover clamp.	14018D	Radiator overflow pipe, upper.
4112D	Water tank handhole cover clamp gasket.	19839D	Radiator inlet elbow gasket.
		19863D	Radiator dust plate.
10161D	Radiator curtain holder.	19875D	Radiator overflow pipe, lower.
10429D	Water tank handhole cover gasket.	19925DX	Radiator curtain, complete.
10629D	Radiator gasket plate, front.	19967D	Radiator, complete.
10634D	Water tank lower stud.	20075D	Radiator outlet hose.
10646DA	Radiator gasket.	20155D	Radiator outlet elbow gasket.
10832D	Radiator overflow pipe clip.	G3277	Radiator drain pipe.
13047DA	Radiator drain pipe cap.		

64

MANIFOLD ASSEMBLY

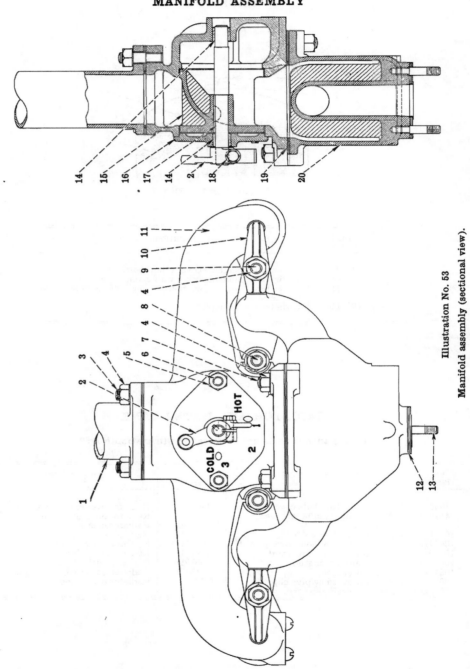

Illustration No. 53

Manifold assembly (sectional view).

MANIFOLD ASSEMBLY

(See illustration No. 53)

Ref. No.	I H C Part No.	DESCRIPTION
1	2340D	Exhaust pipe.
2	19907D	Heat control lever.
3	3060T	Exhaust pipe stud.
4	19962D	Exhaust and intake manifold stud nut.
5	19963D	Exhaust heat control cover stud nut.
6	20667D	Exhaust manifold valve cover stud.
7	G 2436	Intake to exhaust manifold stud ($\frac{1}{2}$ x $1\frac{3}{4}$").
8	14865D	Intake to exhaust manifold stud, short ($\frac{1}{2}$ x $2\frac{3}{16}$").
9	19908D	Exhaust and intake manifold stud, long ($\frac{1}{2}$ x $5\frac{1}{4}$").
10	19909D	Exhaust and intake clamps.
11	2298DX	Exhaust manifold, complete.
12	19906D	Carburetor flange gasket.
13	12215D	Carburetor stud.
14	18741D	Exhaust manifold valve shaft bushing.
15	2295D	Manifold heat control valve.
16	2294DX	Manifold valve cover, complete.
17	19911D	Manifold valve shaft.
18	18761D	Manifold valve lever key ($\frac{3}{4}$ x $\frac{1}{8}$").
19	19912D	Exhaust to intake manifold gasket.
20	2302DX	Intake manifold, complete.

Miscellaneous parts not indicated in illustration No. 53.

I H C Part No.	DESCRIPTION
2418D	Muffler (special).
20588D	Exhaust muffler extension (special).
U14284	Muffler extension clamp (special).

CARBURETOR

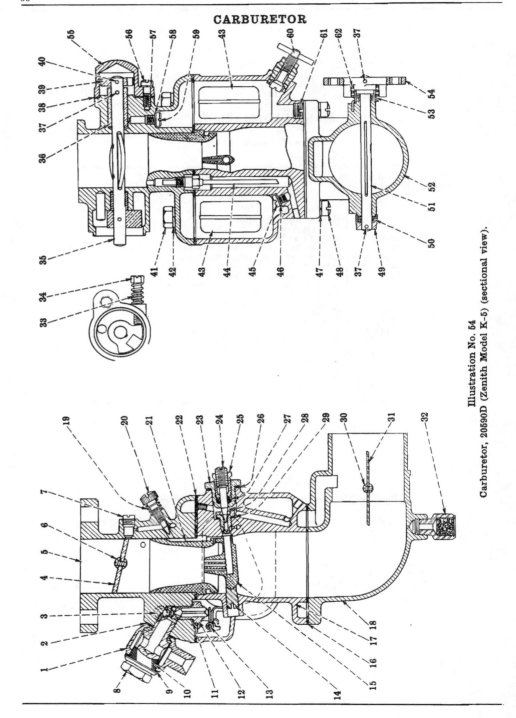

Illustration No. 54

Carburetor, 20590D (Zenith Model K-5) (sectional view).

CARBURETOR

(See illustration No. 54)

Ref. No.	I H C Part No.	Mfr's. No.	DESCRIPTION
1	20060D	D-6774	Union body.
2	13891D	C-71x33	Fiber washer.
3	13861D	C-102	Channel screw.
4	21217D	D-6995	Throttle plate.
5	21201D	A-1194x1	Upper body assembly.
6	12420D	D-3493	Butterfly set screw.
7	20053D	D-6204	Priming hole screw.
8	13570D	D-2422	Union body plug.
9	13892D	C-71x7	Fiber washer.
10	20044D	C-116	Filter screen.
11	12433D	C-71x23	Fiber washer.
12	20058D	D-6560	Fuel valve seat No. 54.
13	21211D	D-5046	Float axle.
14	21229D	D-7174	Nozzle set screw.
15	21220D	D-7137	Nozzle.
16	21228D	D-7152	Intake gasket.
17	21200D	A-1193x1	Bowl assembly.
18	21202D	B-1635	Air intake only.
19	12472D	D-1882	Idle adjustment spring.
20	13873D	D-2566	Idle adjustment needle.
21	21205D	C-4518	Venturi No. 21.
22	21206D	C-4540	Assembly gasket.
23	21222D	D-7139	Packing retainer nut.
24	21223D	D-7140	Adjusting needle.
25	21221D	D-7138	Packing nut.
26	21204D	C-71x6	Fiber washer.
27	21215D	D-6924	Packing.
28	21218D	D-7000	Main jet No. 32.
29	13895D	C-71x12	Fiber washer.
30	13738D	30142	Air shutter screw.
31	16552D	D-5104	Air shutter.
32	21216D	D-6926	Drip plug assembly.
33	12848D	D-4104	Butterfly clamp screw.
34	20203D	D-6892	Butterfly stop screw.
35	21226D	D-7146	Butterfly lever assembly.
36	21225D	D-7144	Economizer valve.
37	12428D	C-42x2	Taper pin.
38	21236D	D-7262	Economizer cap gasket.
39	21235D	D-7261	Throttle driver.
40	21203D	C-42x3	Taper pin.
41	21208D	D-1147	Assembly screw.
42	13876D	D-894	Lockwasher.
43	21227D	D-7323	Float assembly.
44	21214D	D-6371	Idle jet No. 14.
45	18281D	D-1015	Compensator No. 24.
46	12335D	C-71x24	Fiber washer.
47	12459D	D-702	Intake screw lockwasher.
48	21207D	D-449	Intake assembly screw.
49	21232D	D-7258	Packing cap.
50	21210D	D-2204	Packing washer.
51	21212D	D-5744	Air shutter shaft.
52	21213D	6319-M	Intake, complete assembly.
53	12487D	D-2435	Packing ring.
54	21233D	D-7259	Air shutter lever assembly.
55	21224D	D-7143	Economizer cap.
56	12456D	D-453	Cap retaining screw.
57	12404D	D-1197	Lockwasher.
58	12431D	C-71x5	Fiber washer.
59	21209D	D-1561	Economizer No. 12.
60	21231D	D-7256	Drain plug assembly.
61	21234D	D-7260	Pipe plug.
62	20242D	D-4795	Air shutter spring.

68

GOVERNOR

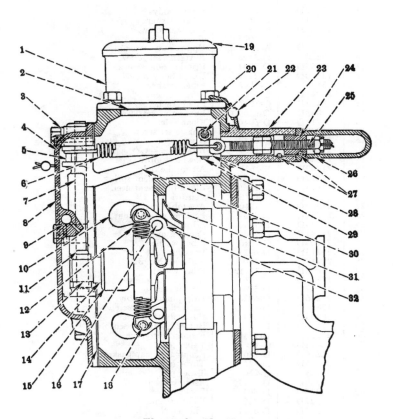

Illustration No. 55
Enclosed governor
(sectional view).

GOVERNOR

(See illustration No. 55.)

Ref. No.	IHC Part No.	DESCRIPTION
1	495D	Oil filler.
2	12727D	Oil filler gasket.
3	4084D	Governor shield cap screw.
4	. . . .	Governor seal.
5	9863T	Governor throttle spring pin.
6	14136D	Governor throttle spring.
7	12710D	Governor rock shaft.
8	582DX	Governor shield with pin.
9	4084D	Governor shield cap screw.
10	12716DX	Governor ball with pin.
11	12711D	Governor shoe pin.
12	12755D	Governor spring.
13	14134D	Governor shoe.
14	. . . .	Governor shoe contact plate (order 1401DDX).
15	1401DDX	Governor sleeve with contact plate.
16	12214D	Governor ball pin.
17	12728D	Governor shield gasket.
18	. . . .	Governor spring pin.
19	101D	Oil filler cap.
20	15208D	Oil filler cap screw.
21	19981D	Governor connecting rod.
22	. . . .	Governor seal.
23	1454D	Governor throttle spring support.
24	14137D	Governor throttle spring adjuster nut.
25	14133D	Governor throttle spring eyebolt.
26	12712DA	Governor throttle spring adjuster.
27	. . . .	Oval head rivet, $\frac{1}{8}$ x $1\frac{1}{4}''$.
28	12719D	Governor connecting rod fork.
29	12715D	Governor fork pivot.
30	12718DX	Governor rock shaft lever, complete.
31	12212D	Governor shield, rear.
32	17220DX	Magneto and governor shaft with carrier.
	17220DY	Magneto and governor shaft, complete with 17220DX.

Miscellaneous parts not indicated in illustration No. 55.

IHC Part No.	DESCRIPTION
438D	Governor gear (28 teeth).
1242DA	Oil filler strainer.
1451D	Governor throttle lever.
2324DX	Governor rod support with bushing.
2383D	Speed change lever.
4098D	Oil filler stud.
11425D	Oil filler screen.
12700D	Governor connecting rod pin ($\frac{1}{4}$ x $1\frac{3}{16}''$).
12724D	Governor rod support bushing.
20000D	Governor rod support cover screw.
20327D	Speed change lever shaft.
20328D	Governor throttle lever pin.
21275D	Governor throttle shaft, complete.
G 1256	Rockshaft lever pivot pin.
3895T	Governor throttle shaft pin.
3895T	Governor speed change lever pin.
6403T	Governor ball carrier dowel.
7225T	Governor gear key.

OIL AIR FILTER (International)

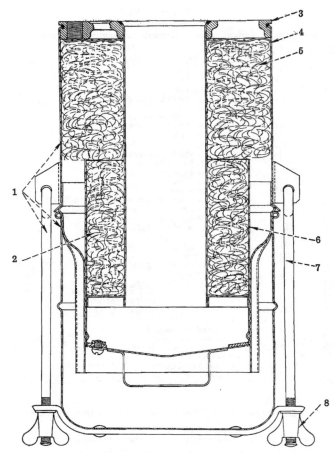

Illustration No. 56—Oil air filter, 19111DX (7″) (sectional view).

Ref. No.	IHC Part No.	DESCRIPTION
1	19111DX	Oil air filter, complete.
2	....	Inlet tube strainer (steel wire).
3	....	Body support.
4	....	Filter body (with strainer).
5	....	Body strainer (steel wire).
6	....	Inlet tube.
7	17975DX	Oil cup clamp rod.
8	11916D	Oil cup wing nut.

OIL AIR FILTER, PIPES AND CONNECTIONS

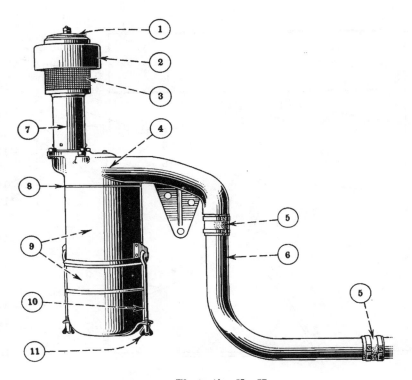

Illustration No. 57

Oil air filter, pipes and connections.

Ref. No.	I H C Part No.	DESCRIPTION
1	17190D	Air pipe screen top reinforcing plate.
2	11196D	Air strainer top.
3	M11948	Air pipe screen.
4	2283D	Air filter top (7″ diam.).
5	11337D	Carburetor connection hose.
6	20601D	Carburetor connection.
7	{15736DX	Air pipe (with flange).
	{15736DY	Air pipe, complete with 15736DX and strainer.
8	19099D	Air filter body gasket.
9	19111DX	Oil air filter, complete, 7″ (International).
10	17975DX	Oil cup clamp rod with nut.
11	11916D	Oil cup wing nut.
		Miscellaneous parts not indicated in illustration No. 57.
......	20035D	Air filter pipe extension.
......	20167DX	Air filter lug ring.
......	G 4944	Air filter top stud.

OIL FILTER (Purolator)

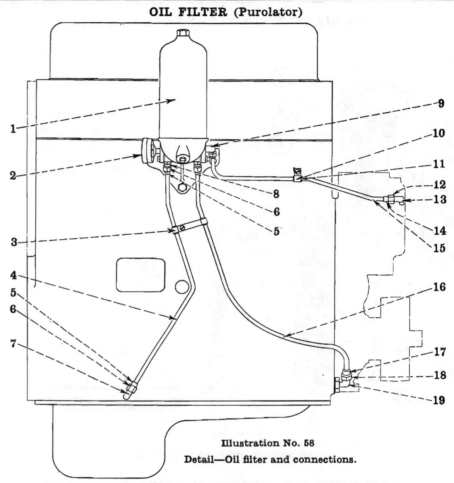

Illustration No. 58

Detail—Oil filter and connections.

Ref. No.	I H C Part No.	DESCRIPTION
1	20682DX	Oil filter (Purolator type "B-29-M").
2	18113D	Oil pressure gauge.
3	16584DA	Oil filter inlet and outlet pipe clip.
4	15952DBX	Oil filter inlet pipe with nut and nipple.
5	16719D	Oil filter inlet pipe nipple.
6	16718D	Oil filter inlet pipe coupling nut.
7	18058D	Oil filter inlet pipe elbow.
8	17241D	Oil filter inlet pipe half union.
9	18057D	Governor oil pipe elbow (long).
10	11659D	Oil pipe clip.
11	11662D	Oil pipe cushion.
12	16715D	Governor oil pipe coupling nut.
13	18060D	Governor oil pipe elbow.
14	16716D	Governor oil pipe coupling nipple.
15	15954DCX	Governor oil pipe with nut and nipple.
16	15953DCX	Oil filter outlet pipe with nut and nipple.
17	16719D	Oil filter outlet pipe nipple.
18	16718D	Oil filter outlet pipe coupling nut.
19	18058D	Oil filter outlet pipe elbow.
......	17241D	Oil filter outlet pipe half union.

OIL FILTER (Purolator)

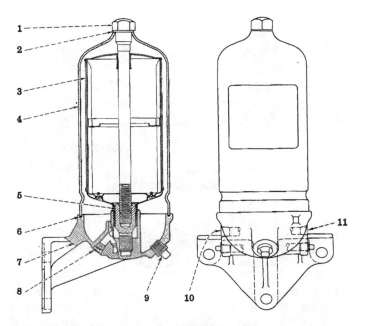

Illustration No. 59—Oil filter, 20682DX (sectional view).

Ref. No.	I H C Part No.	DESCRIPTION
1	21290D	Retaining stud.
2	13727D	Retaining stud gasket.
3	21288D	Element assembly (metal element).
4	13729D	Case.
5	21291D	Retaining stud adapter.
6	13728DA	Case gasket.
7	21289D	Base assembly.
8	....	Inlet.
9	....	Drain plug.
10	....	Inlet for gauge.
11	....	Outlet.

MAGNETO

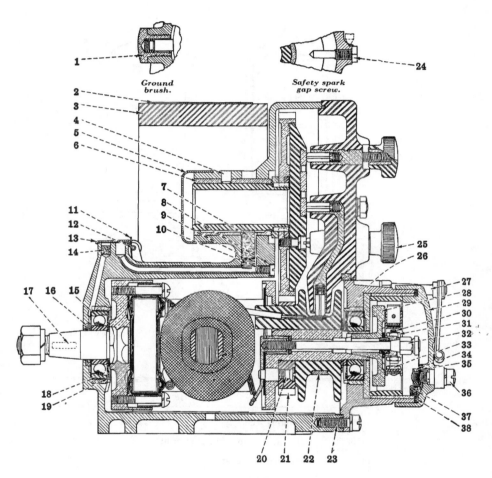

1

Ground brush.

2
3
4
5
6

7
8
9
10

11
12
13
14

17 16 15

18
19

24

Safety spark gap screw.

25
26

27
28
29
30
31
32
33
34
35

36

37
38

20 21 22 23

Illustration No. 60

Side view of E4A magneto assembly (sectional).

MAGNETO

(See illustration No. 60.)

Ref. No.	IHC Part No.	DESCRIPTION	Ref. No.	IHC Part No.	DESCRIPTION
1	E4 -218	Ground brush holder.	22	E4A-522	Collector ring.
2	E4A-28A	Name plate and magneto band.	23	E4A-358	Magneto end plate and breaker housing screw, plain.
3	E4 -1	Magnet.			
4	E4A-473	Dowel pin for distributor gear shaft bushing.	24	E4 -244	Safety spark gap screw.
5	E4A-233B	Distributor gear shaft cover.	25	E4A-320	Distributor block thumb nut.
6	E4A-231	Distributor gear shaft bushing.	26	E4A-325	Oil flinger spacer.
7	E4A-217	Distributor gear shaft oil wick.	27	E4A-314A	Breaker housing cover spring post, complete (specify magneto number when ordering).
8	E4A-321	Magneto distributor shaft oil pipe screw gasket.			
9	E4A-247	Distributor gear shaft oil wick spring.	28	E4A-304A	Breaker, complete with breaker points.
10	E4A-322	Magneto distributor shaft oil pipe screw.	29	E4A-284AY	Breaker housing cover, complete.
11	E4 -245	Magneto frame oil well cover spring.	30	E4A-258 / E4A-258Y	Fixed breaker point. / Fixed breaker point with lock nut.
12	E4 -225	Magneto frame oil well cover pin.	31	E4A-262	Fixed breaker point lock nut.
13	E4 -224	Magneto frame oil well cover.	32	E4 -229A	Breaker screw for holding breaker in place.
14	E4 -216	Ball bearing oil well felt.	33	E4A-552X	Breaker arm point.
15	E4 -261	Bearing insulation, outer.	34	E4A-499	Short-circuiting terminal inside nut.
16	E4 -226	Magneto bearing felt.	35	E4A-307A	Short-circuiting terminal insulation.
17	4167T	Key for armature driving end.	36	E4A-503	Short-circuiting terminal screw, short.
18	E4 -294	Magneto shaft ball bearing, complete.			
19	E4A-324	Oil flinger.	37	E4A-275A	Short-circuiting spring, outer.
20	E4A-461	Armature pinion screw.	38	E4A-302	Breaker housing cover packing.
21	E4 -207	Armature pinion, 37 teeth.			

Miscellaneous parts not indicated in illustration No. 60.

IHC Part No.	DESCRIPTION	IHC Part No.	DESCRIPTION
19397DA	Magneto cover, complete.	E4A-333AX	Short-circuiting spring, inner, complete.
E4A- 5AX	Magneto end plate and breaker housing.	E4A-347A	Magneto, complete with automatic impulse coupling.
E4A- 76X	Distributor brush, complete with spring.	E4A-351	Inner race for magneto shaft ball bearing.
E4A-105	Magneto frame, complete.	E4A-352	Outer race for magneto shaft ball bearing.
E4A-150A	Armature assembly, complete with winding and condenser.	E4A-353	Retainer (with balls) for magneto shaft ball bearing.
E4A-200	Magneto, complete (less impulse coupling.)	E4A-366X	Distributor block screw, complete (specify magneto number when ordering).
E4 -214	Breaker cam felt.		
E4A-263	Bearing insulation, rear.	E4A-471AX	Breaker cam, complete (specify magneto number when ordering).
E4A-265X	Distributor disk with screws and lockwashers.	E4A-476	Distributor block felt, lower.
E4A-270AX	Distributor block with 2 felts (less thumb nuts).	E4A-477	Distributor block felt, upper.
E4A-270AY	Distributor block, complete with thumb nuts.	E4A-559	Breaker, complete (less breaker points) (specify magneto number when ordering).
E4A-284A	Breaker housing cover.		
E4A-289X	Magneto wrench with gauges.	E4A-576	Ball bearing oil well felt.
E4 -295	Oiler for armature shaft.	O 37	Magneto band screw.
E4A-303A	Collector ring lockwasher.		
E4A-318AX	Distributor gear with shaft and disk.		

BREAKER ASSEMBLY

(for E4A Magneto)

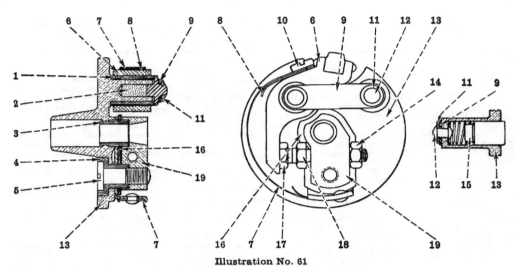

Illustration No. 61

Breaker assembly, E4A-304A (Pivoted Arm Type)

(for E4A Magneto) (sectional view).

Ref. No.	I H C Part No.	DESCRIPTION
1	E4A-536	Breaker arm bushing.
2	E4A-539	Breaker arm post felt.
3	E4A-551	Breaker center bushing.
4	E4A-550	Stationary point support bushing.
5	E4A-549	Stationary point support screw.
6	E4A-558X	Breaker arm with bushing.
	E4A-558Y	Breaker arm with point and bushing.
7	E4A-543X	Breaker arm spring post with spring.
8	E4A-555	Breaker arm reinforcing spring, short.
9	E4A-541X	Breaker arm cap spring with cap.
10	E4A-546	Breaker spring screw.
11	E4A-542	Breaker arm cap spring washer.
12	E4A-570	Breaker arm cap spring rivet.
13	E4A-557X	Breaker carrier with spring and cap.
14	E4A-262	Fixed breaker point lock nut.
15	E4A-554X	Ground brush with spring.
16	E4A-548	Stationary point support insulation.
17	E4A-552X	Breaker arm point.
18	E4A-258Y	Fixed breaker point with lock nut.
19	E4A-547	Stationary point support.

INTERNATIONAL AUTOMATIC IMPULSE COUPLING (E4A-500)
(for E4A Magneto)

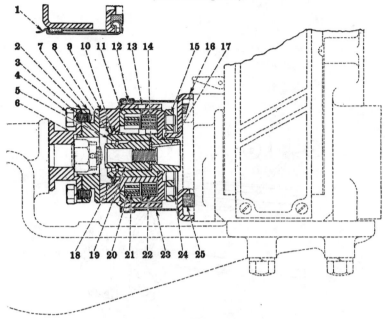

Illustration No. 62
Automatic impulse coupling, E4A-500 (for E4A Magneto) (sectional view).

Ref. No.	I H C Part No.	DESCRIPTION
1	E4A-439	Cover spring.
2	10481D	Magneto coupling shim, medium.
	10482D	Magneto coupling shim, heavy.
	10553D	Magneto coupling shim, light.
3	. . . .	Lockwasher, $\frac{1}{4}$".
4	. . . .	Cap screw, $\frac{1}{4}$ x $\frac{3}{8}$".
5	E4A-451B	Magneto member, complete.
6	7882T	Magneto coupling.
7	12740D	Magneto coupling block, male.
8	E4A-453	Magneto member shaft snap ring, outer.
9	12741D	Magneto coupling block spacer.
10	E4A-452	Magneto member shaft outer snap ring washer.
11	E4A-456	Coupling member stop ring.
12	E4A-437	Cover felt.
13	E4A-447C	Coupling member, complete.
14	. . . .	Lockwasher, $\frac{7}{16}$" (special light).
15	E4A-440	Pawl.
16	E4A-434	Coupling plate.
17	4167T	Key for magneto member.
18	E4A-454	Magneto member shaft snap ring, inner.
19	E4A-455	Coupling nut.
20	E4A-572	Snubber spring felt.
21	E4A-460	Snubber spring.
22	E4A-459	Drive spring.
23	E4A-438	Coupling cover, complete.
24	E4A-442	Pawl pin snap ring.
25	E4A-457	Coupling plate felt.
. . . . . .	E4A-500	Automatic impulse coupling, complete.
. . . . . .	E4A-583	Impulse coupling rotating unit, complete.

SPARK PLUG CABLE ASSEMBLY

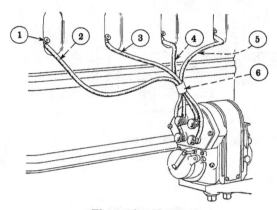

Illustration No. 63

Spark plug cable assembly.

Ref. No.	I H C Part No.	DESCRIPTION
1	13117D	Spark plug, $\frac{7}{8}''$ (Champion No. 1).
2	12747D	No. 4 spark plug cable.
3	14042D	No. 3 spark plug cable.
4	4672D	No. 2 spark plug cable.
5	4675D	No. 1 spark plug cable.
6	10435DB	Spark plug cable assembly.

FUEL TANK AND VALVE CONNECTIONS

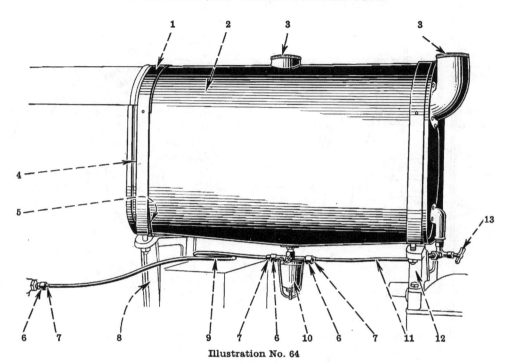

Illustration No. 64

Fuel tank and valve connections.

Ref. No.	IHC Part No.	DESCRIPTION
1	19871D	Fuel tank strap, complete.
2	19872DX	Fuel and gas tank, complete with caps.
3	11446D	Fuel tank cap assembly.
4	15123DA	Fuel tank pad.
5	19968D	Fuel tank strap lining.
6	16718D	Fuel pipe coupling nuts.
7	16719D	Fuel pipe coupling nipples.
8	2281D	Fuel tank bracket, front.
9	20602DX	Fuel pipe to carburetor, complete with nuts.
10	17237D	Fuel strainer assembly.
11	19885DX	Fuel pipe, gas tank to strainer, complete with nuts.
12	2282D	Fuel tank bracket, rear.
13	17228D	Shut-off needle valve.
		Miscellaneous parts not indicated in illustration No. 64.
	11659D	Fuel pipe clip.
	11662D	Fuel pipe cushion.
	17241D	Half union (fuel line to carburetor.)

CLUTCH (12″)

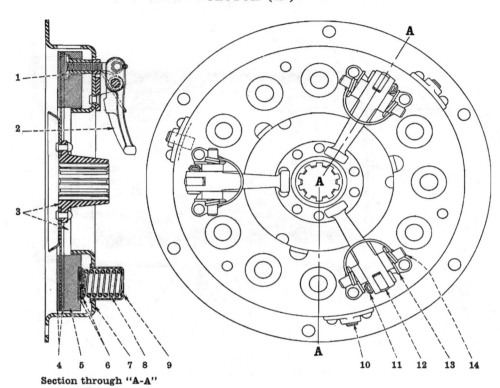

Section through "A-A"

Illustration No. 65—Single plate clutch (14611D) (sectional view).

Ref. No.	I H C Part No.	DESCRIPTION	Ref. No.	I H C Part No.	DESCRIPTION
1	12989D	Release lever eye-bolt sleeve.	8	14909D	Clutch pressure spring.
2	14618DA	Release lever.	9	12981D	Clutch pressure plate spring cup.
3	14624D	Clutch driven disk and facing.	10	12983D	Clutch pressure plate driving pin.
4	14622DA	Friction facing.	11	16881D	Release lever eye-bolt pin.
5	987D	Clutch pressure plate.	12	12982DA	Release lever eye-bolt.
6	14603DB	Pressure spring insulating cup.	13	16885D	Release lever spring.
7	14623DX	Clutch cover plate, complete.	14	16882D	Release lever pin.

CLUTCH AND CONNECTING PARTS

Miscellaneous parts not indicated in illustration No. 65.

I H C Part No.	DESCRIPTION	I H C Part No.	DESCRIPTION
2278D	Clutch pedal.	14186D	Clutch housing cap lubricator (Zerk).
11537D	Clutch pedal spring.		
12366D	Clutch shifter rod fork.	14611D	Clutch, complete (12″).
13129D	Clutch release bearing lubricator (Zerk).	14753D	Release sleeve pivot pin.
13129D	Clutch shifter shaft lubricator (Zerk).	15817D	Clutch pedal spring holder.
13199D	Clutch release bearing oil tube coupling elbow.	2015T	Clutch shifter rod fork pin.

CLUTCH AND TRANSMISSION COUPLING ASSEMBLY

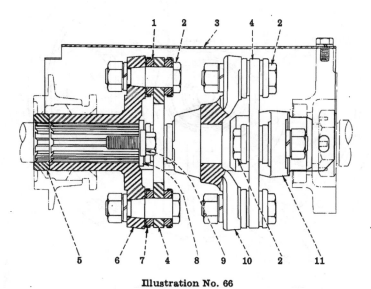

Illustration No. 66

Clutch and transmission coupling assembly (sectional view).

Ref. No.	I H C Part No.	DESCRIPTION
1	19853D	Clutch joint rubber washer.
2	19855DX	Clutch joint screw, complete.
3	19926D	Clutch joint shield.
4	19862D	Clutch joint ring.
5	19861D	Transmission joint sleeve.
6	19860D	Transmission shaft joint.
7	19854D	Clutch joint rubber washer retainer.
8	19852D	Transmission joint washer.
9	20274D	Transmission joint lock plate.
10	19859D	Clutch joint coupling.
11	19858D	Clutch shaft joint.

82

CLUTCH AND HOUSING ASSEMBLY

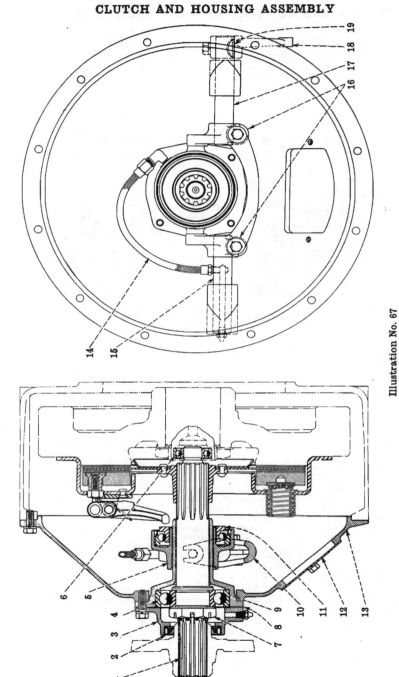

Illustration No. 67

Clutch and housing assembly (sectional view).

CLUTCH AND HOUSING ASSEMBLY

(See illustration No. 67)

Ref. No.	I H C Part No.	DESCRIPTION
1	19919D	Clutch shaft.
2	18100D	Clutch shaft bearing oil seal.
3	2315D	Clutch housing cap.
4	20158D	Clutch shaft ball bearing, rear.
5	2312D	Clutch release sleeve.
	2312DX	Clutch release sleeve, complete with pin and rivets.
6	10701DA	Clutch shaft ball bearing, front.
7	4591D	Clutch shaft nut.
8	19953D	Clutch housing cap gasket.
9	2313DX	Clutch shaft retainer, complete.
10	2314D	Clutch shifter fork.
11	13149D	Clutch throw-out bearing.
12	13698VA	Clutch housing hand hole cover.
13	2316D	Clutch housing.
14	15946DX	Clutch release bearing oil tube, complete.
15	19920D	Clutch shifter shaft.
16	14026D	Clutch shifter shaft key.
17	19921D	Clutch lever shaft.
18	1533DB	Clutch lever.
19	10430V	Clutch lever key.

TRANSMISSION ASSEMBLY

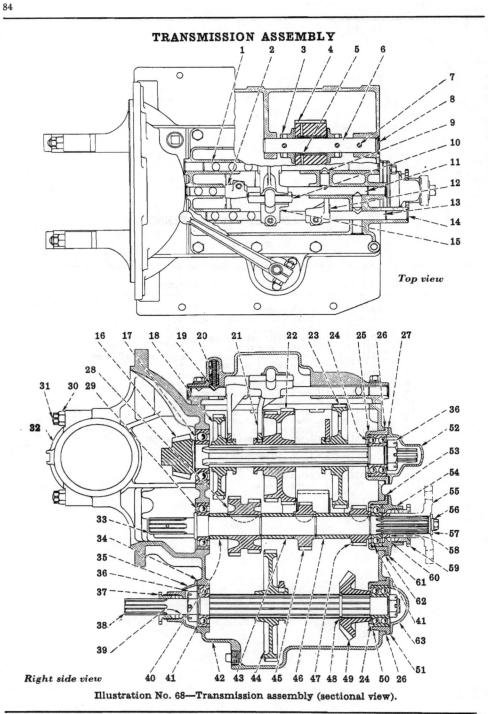

Top view

Right side view

Illustration No. 68—Transmission assembly (sectional view).

TRANSMISSION ASSEMBLY
(See illustration No. 68.)

Ref. No.	I H C Part No.	DESCRIPTION
1	19815D	Second and third speed shifter shaft.
2	19821D	Fourth speed shifter fork.
3	2263D	Reverse gear thrust collar.
4	19768DX	Reverse gear, complete.
5	19778D	Reverse gear bushing.
6	19775D	Power take-off shifter shaft.
7	19779DA	Reverse gear shaft bolt ($\frac{5}{16}$ x 2$\frac{3}{4}$").
8	13062D	Transmission case expansion plug.
9	19826D	Shifter shaft inter-locking plug.
10	19819D	Fourth speed shifter socket.
11	19816D	Fourth speed shifter shaft.
12	19822D	First and reverse speed shifter fork.
13	19817D	First and reverse speed shifter shaft.
14	17562D	Transmission case cover expansion plug (1").
15	19820D	First and reverse shifter socket.
16	19771D	Transmission spline shaft and bevel pinion (14 teeth).
17	12797H	Spline shaft ball bearing, rear, complete.
18	19811D	Fourth speed sliding gear (42 teeth).
19	9222H	Gear shift poppet.
20	10862D	Gear shift poppet spring.
21	19818D	Second and third speed shifter fork.
22	19766D	Second and third speed sliding gear (45 and 48 teeth).
23	19765D	Low speed sliding gear (52 teeth).
24	13188D	Spline shaft ball bearing, front, complete. / Power take-off shaft ball bearing, front, complete.
25	2255D	Transmission spline shaft bearing retainer.
26	19786D / 19786D / 19787D / 19787D	Spline shaft and bevel pinion bearing retainer shim, heavy (.0156"). / Power take-off shaft bearing retainer shim, heavy (.0156"). / Spline shaft and bevel pinion bearing retainer shim, light (.007"). / Power take-off shaft bearing retainer shim, light (.007").
27	20105D	Spline shaft ball bearing retainer gasket.
28	19764D	Third and fourth speed pinions (26 and 29 teeth).
29	14225H	Transmission shaft ball bearing, rear, complete.
30	19799D	Transmission case stud nut.
31	19798D	Transmission case stud ($\frac{3}{4}$ x 5$\frac{3}{8}$").
32	2266D	Differential ball bearing cap.
33	19772D	Transmission shaft.
34	19796D	Power take-off stuffing box gasket.
35	2260D	Power take-off shaft stuffing box.
36	19825D	Spline shaft nut. / Power take-off shaft nut.
37	2262D	Power take-off shaft packing gland.
38	19773D	Power take-off shaft.
39	19784D	Power take-off shaft packing.
40	19780D	Transmission shaft gear spacer, short.
41	14226H / 14226H	Power take-off shaft ball bearing, rear, complete. / Transmission shaft ball bearing, front, complete.
42	2254DX	Transmission case, complete.
43	19781D	Transmission shaft gear spacer (medium).
44	19767D	Power take-off gear (56 teeth).
45	19763D	Second speed pinion (34 teeth).
46	19782D	Transmission shaft gear spacer, long.
47	19762D	Low speed pinion (19 teeth).
48	11705D	Power take-off shaft split collar.
49	19770D	Power take-off shaft bevel gear (23 teeth).
50	2287D	Power take-off shaft bearing retainer.
51	19795D	Power take-off shaft bearing retainer cap gasket.
52	2308D	Spline shaft bearing retainer cap.
53	2256D	Transmission shaft bearing retainer.
54	2258D	Transmission shaft stuffing box.
55	19860D	Transmission shaft joint.
56	20274D	Transmission joint lock plate.
57	19852D	Transmission joint washer.
58	19861D	Transmission joint sleeve.
59	2261D	Transmission shaft packing gland.
60	19831D	Transmission shaft packing.
61	19794D	Transmission stuffing box gasket.
62	19793D	Transmission shaft ball bearing retainer gasket.
63	2257D	Power take-off bearing retainer cap.

TRANSMISSION ASSEMBLY

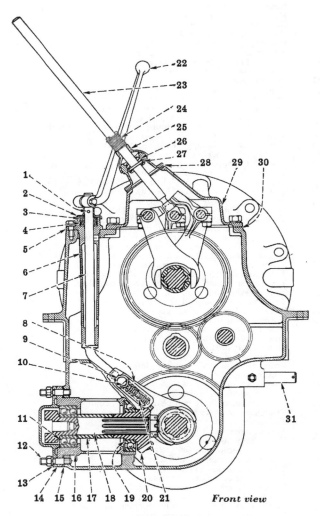

Front view

Illustration No. 69
Transmission assembly (sectional view).

TRANSMISSION ASSEMBLY

(See illustration No. 69.)

Ref. No.	IHC Part No.	DESCRIPTION
1	19807D	Power take-off shifter lever pin ($\frac{3}{16}$ x $1\frac{1}{8}$").
2	19805D	Power take-off shifter lever cap.
3	19813D	Power take-off shifter felt washer.
4	19812D	Power take-off shifter bearing oil seal.
5	19808D	Power take-off shifter shaft bearing gasket.
6	2265DX	Power take-off shifter shaft bearing, complete.
7	19804DA	Power take-off shifter lever, complete.
8	19809D	Power take-off shifter fork.
9	19775D	Power take-off shifter shaft.
10	9222H	Power take-off shifter poppet.
11	13188D	Belt pulley shaft ball bearing.
12	19969D	Belt pulley inner carrier inner stud ($\frac{1}{2}$ x $2\frac{7}{16}$").
13	2269D	Belt pulley bearing cap.
14	20032D	Belt pulley inner carrier gasket.
15	19790D	Belt pulley carrier shim, heavy (.0156").
	19791D	Belt pulley carrier shim, light (.007").
16	2264D	Belt pulley carrier, inner.
17	19785D	Belt pulley carrier bearing spacer.
18	19776D	Belt pulley shaft, inner.
19	14234H	Belt pulley ball bearing, inner, complete.
20	19769D	Belt pulley pinion (18 teeth).
21	10862H	Power take-off shifter poppet spring.
22	2333D	Power take-off shift hand lever.
23	15047DA	Gear shift lever.
24	15278D	Gear shift lever spring.
25	1518DCX	Gear shift ball socket cap.
26	15021D	Gear shift lever ball.
27	G 9210	Gear shift lever ball pin.
28	2268D	Gear shift ball socket.
29	2267DX	Transmission case cover, complete.
30	19823D	Transmission case cover gasket.
31	19847D	Clutch pedal shaft.

Miscellaneous parts not indicated in illustrations No. 68 and 69.

IHC Part No.	DESCRIPTION
17562D	Transmission case cover expansion plug (1").
19514D	Transmission, complete.
19774D	Reverse shaft.
19779DA	Reverse gear shaft thrust collar bolt ($\frac{5}{16}$ x $2\frac{3}{4}$").
19788D	Power take-off shifter lever key.
19800D	Transmission shaft packing gland lock.
19801D	Power take-off shaft packing gland lock.
19802D	Transmission case flange stud.
19810D	Power take-off shifter shaft locking screw.
19824D	Gear shift ball socket gasket.
19960D	Third and fourth speed pinion key.
19961D	Second speed pinion key.
19961D	Low speed pinion key.
20168D	Gear shift ball socket cap bushing.

DIFFERENTIAL ASSEMBLY

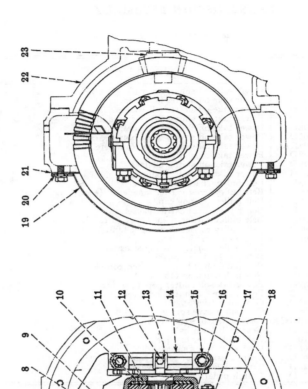

Illustration No. 70

Differential assembly (sectional view).

DIFFERENTIAL ASSEMBLY

(See illustration No. 70.)

Ref. No.	I H C Part No.	DESCRIPTION
1	19755D	Countershaft.
2	2251DX	Countershaft housing.
3	2234D	Differential ball bearing retainer.
4	19892D	Differential ball bearing.
5	2235D	Differential ball bearing retainer adjusting nut.
6	19888D	Differential bevel gear (26 teeth).
7	19897D	Bevel gear oil wiper.
8	19890DX	Differential case (right half with left).
9	19886D	Differential spider.
10	19895D	Differential thrust washer dowel pin ($\frac{5}{16}$ x $\frac{3}{4}''$).
11	19894D	Differential bevel gear thrust washer.
12	15527D	Differential ball bearing retainer screw lock.
13	19891D	Differential ball bearing retainer lock screw.
14	2266D	Differential ball bearing cap.
15	19799D	Transmission case stud nut.
16	19887D	Differential pinion (14 teeth).
17	19893DX	Differential case bolt, complete.
18	19896D	Bevel ring gear (60 teeth).
19	19757D	Countershaft housing cover.
20	19758D	Countershaft housing cover ring.
21	19759D	Countershaft housing cover gasket.
22	2254DX	Transmission case, complete.
23	19771D	Transmission spline shaft and bevel pinion (14 teeth).

BELT PULLEY AND CARRIER ASSEMBLY

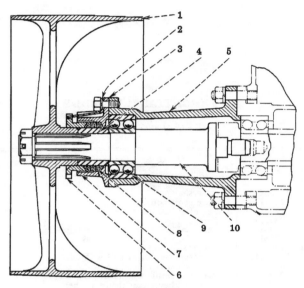

Illustration No. 71

Belt pulley and carrier assembly (sectional view).

Ref. No.	I H C Part No.	DESCRIPTION
1	2272DX	Belt pulley with weights (14⅝" diam., 7" face).
2	19800D	Belt pulley packing gland lock.
3	19797D	Belt pulley stuffing box gasket.
4	19856D	Belt pulley spacer.
5	2271D	Belt pulley carrier, outer.
6	2261D	Belt pulley shaft packing gland.
7	2270D	Belt pulley stuffing box.
8	19831D	Belt pulley shaft packing.
9	13188D	Belt pulley ball bearing, outer.
10	19830D	Belt pulley shaft, outer.

FRONT AXLE AND WHEELS

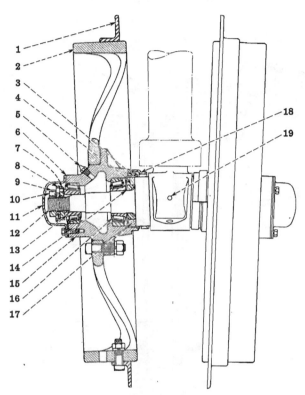

Illustration No. 72
Front axle and wheels (sectional view).

Ref. No.	I H C Part No.	DESCRIPTION
1	15360DB	Front wheel tire ring.
2	2240D	Front wheel (25″ diam. x 4″ face) (less tire ring).
3	19712DX	Front wheel oil seal retainer, complete.
4	19709D	Front wheel bearing spacer.
5	14186D	Front wheel lubricator (Zerk).
6	10828D	Front wheel hub cap gasket.
7	12305DX	Front axle nut, complete.
8	12308D	Front axle adjusting lock.
9	12307D	Front axle nut lock.
10	12311D	Front axle locking nut.
11	12312D	Front wheel hub cap.
12	20605DX	Front axle, complete.
13	13200DA	Front wheel roller bearing outer, complete.
14	19714D	Front wheel felt washer retainer, inner.
15	2239DX	Front wheel hub, complete.
16	13386D	Front wheel roller bearing, inner, complete.
17	19713D	Front wheel felt washer.
18	19710DX	Front wheel dust shield, complete.
19	15201D	Front axle pin ($\frac{3}{8}$ x $2\frac{7}{8}$″).

FRONT AXLE, SHAFT, STEERING GEAR AND STARTING CRANK

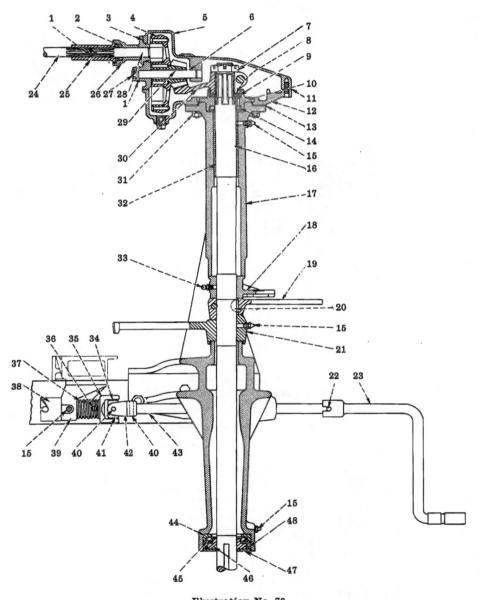

Illustration No. 73

Front axle, shaft, steering gear and starting crank (sectional view).

FRONT AXLE, SHAFT, STEERING GEAR AND STARTING CRANK

(See illustration No. 73)

Ref. No.	I H C Part No.	DESCRIPTION	Ref. No.	I H C Part No.	DESCRIPTION
1	G 2855	Steering bevel pinion shaft pin ($\frac{3}{16}$ x $1\frac{1}{2}$").	26	2238DX	Steering spur pinion bearing.
2	19707D	Steering shaft oil seal.	27	13090D	Steering gear case cover expansion plug.
3	19705D	Steering spur pinion bearing gasket.	28	19696D	Steering spur pinion (10 teeth).
4	20106DX	Steering gear hub with gear and pinion, complete.	29	19701D	Steering bevel pinion bushing.
			30	19694D	Steering sector (16 teeth).
5	2236DX	Steering gear case cover, complete.	31	20154D	Steering gear case stud.
6	19697D	Steering bevel pinion shaft.	32	15139D	Front axle shaft support bushing.
7	4647D	Front axle shaft nut.	33	13129D	Front axle shaft spacer cap lubricator (Zerk).
8	{15096D 15097D}	Steering sector shim, light (.007"). Steering sector shim, heavy (.0156").	34	15272D	Starting crank knuckle gimbal pin, large.
9	20284D	Steering sector thrust washer.	35	1573D	Starting crank knuckle, rear.
10	2367DX	Front axle shaft oil seal retainer, complete.	36	G3754	Starting crank knuckle pin ($\frac{5}{16}$ x $1\frac{1}{2}$").
11	19699D	Steering gear case cover gasket.	37	15274D	Starting crank spring.
12	2237DX	Steering gear case, complete.	38	15273D	Starting crank ratchet.
13	19706D	Steering gear case gasket.	39	2280D	Starting crank bearing.
14	19702D	Front axle shaft oil seal.	40	2709T	Starting crank gimbal pin, small.
15	14186D	Lubricator fitting (Zerk).	41	1574D	Starting crank knuckle gimbal.
16	20605DX	Front axle, complete.	42	1572D	Starting crank knuckle, front.
17	2279DX	Front bolster, complete.	43	15162DB	Starting crankshaft.
18	1553DAX	Front axle shaft spacer, complete.	44	15054D	Front axle shaft bearing outer race.
19	15107D	Cultivator shifter lever.	45	13087D	Front axle shaft bearing ball.
20	13089D	Cultivator shifter lever key.	46	15305D	Front axle shaft bearing inner race and felt retainer.
21	15108DC	Countershaft brake cable lever.	47	15057D	Front axle shaft felt washer retainer washer.
22	15204D	Starting crank pin.	48	15055D	Front axle shaft felt washer.
23	15179DAX	Starting crank, complete.			
24	19882D	Steering shaft.			
25	19704D	Steering shaft coupling.			

FRONT AXLE AND WHEELS, STEERING GEAR AND STARTING CRANK

Miscellaneous parts not indicated in illustrations Nos. 72 and 73.

I H C Part No.	DESCRIPTION
13063D	Steering wheel key (Woodruff).
13201D	Front wheel roller bearing cup.
13205DA	Front wheel roller bearing cone, complete.
13207D	Front wheel roller bearing cup.
13391D	Front wheel roller bearing cone, complete.
14177D	Throttle hand lever stop pin ($\frac{3}{16}$ x 1").
14187D	Steering shaft bearing lubricator (Zerk).
14187D	Steering spur pinion bearing lubricator (Zerk).
15545D	Steering shaft bearing pin ($\frac{1}{4}$ x $2\frac{7}{16}$").
19700D	Steering gear pin ($\frac{1}{4}$ x $1\frac{5}{16}$").
19703D	Steering gear case dowel pin.
19715D	Front axle shaft key ($\frac{7}{16}$ x $4\frac{7}{8}$").
20504D	Starting crank bearing stud.

REAR WHEEL AND COUNTERSHAFT BRAKE ASSEMBLY

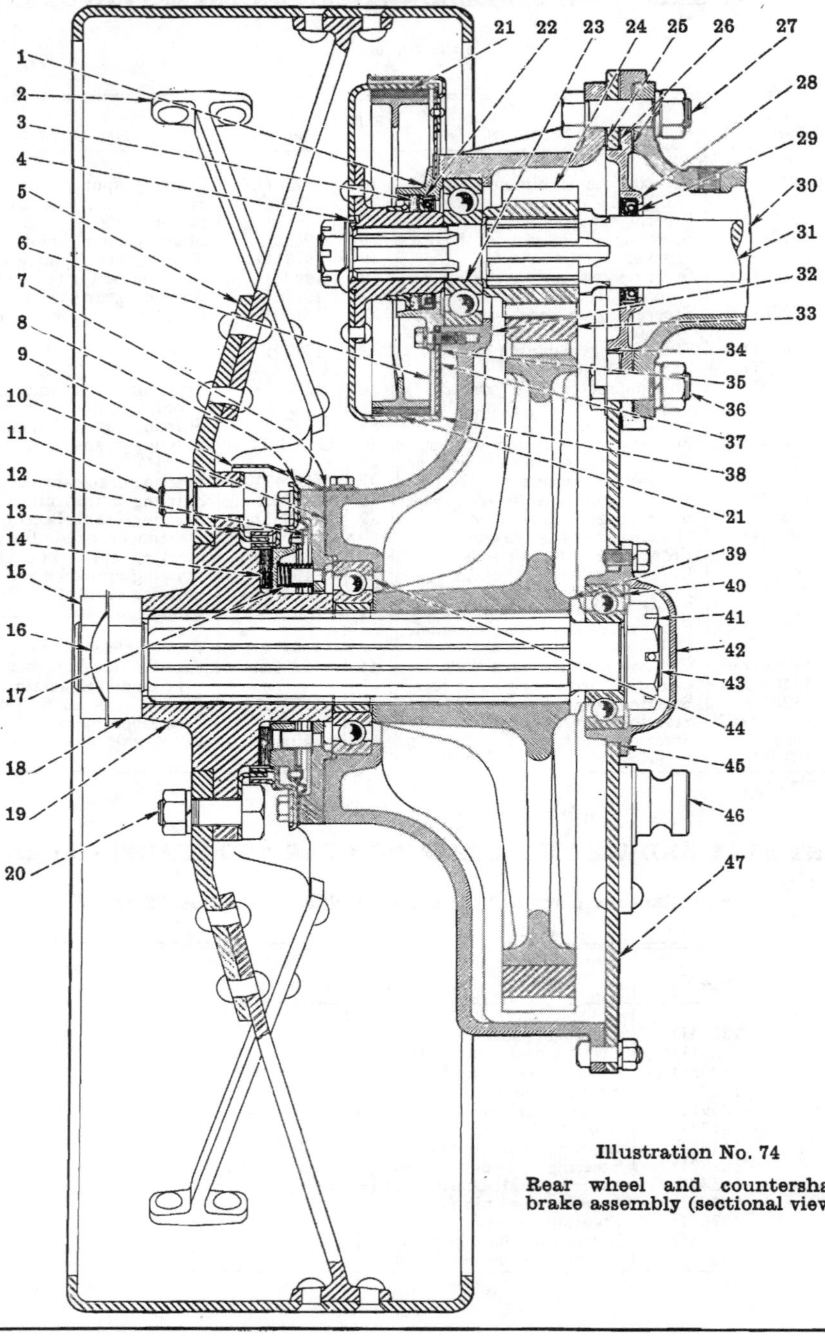

Illustration No. 74

Rear wheel and countershaft brake assembly (sectional view).

REAR WHEEL AND COUNTERSHAFT BRAKE ASSEMBLY

(See illustration No. 74.)

Ref. No.	I H C Part No.	DESCRIPTION
1	2249DX	Countershaft ball bearing retainer, complete.
2	20174D	Rear wheel spoke.
3	19744D	Countershaft felt washer.
4	19737D	Countershaft nut lock.
5	20256D	Rear wheel hub.
6	2246DX	Countershaft brake shoe, inner, complete.
	2247DX	Countershaft brake shoe, outer, complete.
7	19734D	Rear axle outer bearing retainer gasket.
8	19726DX	Oil seal guard, complete.
9	19727D	Rear axle dirt shield.
10	2245DX	Rear axle outer bearing retainer, complete.
11	19844DX	Rear wheel hub dowel bolt, complete.
12	19725DX.	Rear axle oil seal diaphragm.
13	19866D	Rear wheel hub carrier ring.
14	19728D	Oil seal packing.
15	12801D	Rear axle check nut ($2\frac{1}{4}''$).
16	19733D	Rear axle nut lockwasher.
17	17383D	Rear axle oil seal spring.
18	12800D	Rear axle nut ($2\frac{1}{4}''$).
19	19723D	Rear wheel hub carrier.
20	19732DX	Rear wheel hub bolt, complete.
21	19741D	Countershaft brake shoe lining.
22	19761D	Countershaft oil seal, outer.
23	8355H	Countershaft ball bearing.
24	19745D	Drive pinion (15 teeth).
25	19749D	Rear axle carrier gasket.
26	19750D	Countershaft housing end gasket.
27	19754DX	Rear axle carrier dowel bolt, complete.
28	2250DX	Countershaft housing end, complete.
29	19760D	Countershaft oil seal, inner.
30	2251DX	Countershaft housing, complete.
31	19755D	Countershaft.
32	2241DX	Rear axle carrier, complete.
33	2243DX	Drive gear hub with gear, complete.
34	19753D	Rear axle carrier plate dowel bolt lock.
35	19746D	Countershaft ball bearing retainer gasket.
36	19752DX	Countershaft housing bolt, complete.
37	19742DX	Brake shoe and drum mud shield, complete.
38	2248DX	Countershaft brake drum and hub, complete.
39	19720D	Rear axle spacer.
40	12797H	Rear axle inner bearing.
41	19718D	Rear axle inner nut ($3''$ hex. x $1''$).
42	2242D	Rear axle inner bearing retainer.
43	19721DX	Rear axle, complete.
44	19735D	Rear axle outer bearing.
45	19717D	Rear axle inner bearing retainer gasket.
46	19722D	Draw bar pivot pin.
47	19965D	Rear axle carrier plate, L. H., complete.
	19966D	Rear axle carrier plate, R. H., complete.

REAR AXLE, REAR WHEEL AND COUNTERSHAFT

Miscellaneous parts not indicated in illustration No. 74.

I H C Part No.	DESCRIPTION
1551DA	Countershaft brake sheave.
2252D	Countershaft brake lever.
11095DA	Spade lug (5″).
13083D	Oil seal pressure plate inner plug.
13110D	Countershaft brake cable shackle, complete.
13687D	Countershaft brake lever key.
14186D	Countershaft brake cable lever lubricator (Zerk).
15020DB	Hand brake lever ratchet.
15136DB	Countershaft brake sheave spacer.
15199D	Countershaft brake shoe spring.
15269DA	Countershaft brake sheave shield.
15346D	Hand brake ratchet fork pin ($\frac{1}{2}$ x $1\frac{7}{8}$″).
15416D	Hand brake ratchet spring.
15524D	Differential ball bearing retainer adjusting nut lock.
15585D	Countershaft brake shoe pin wick.
17106D	Rear axle oil seal spring centering pin.
17107D	Rear axle oil seal pressure plate driving stud.
17682DA	Countershaft brake cable shackle.
17683D	Countershaft brake cable shackle pin.
19729D	Oil seal diaphragm ring.
19730D	Oil seal pressure plate, inner.
19740D	Countershaft brake shoe wearing plate.
19743DX	Countershaft brake shoe pin, complete.
19751DX	Rear axle carrier plate dowel bolt, complete.
19756D	Brake camshaft.
19802D	Transmission case stud.
19828DX	Transmission case flange bolt, complete.
19829D	Transmission case flange bolt lock.
19833D	Brake cable spring adjusting nut.
19834D	Countershaft brake lever spring, L. H.
19835D	Countershaft brake lever spring, R. H.
20101D	Brake drum hub collar.
20175DA	Rear wheel, complete, less lugs (12″).
20216D	Transmission case flange gasket.

8″ REAR WHEEL ATTACHMENT (20176D) (Special)

I H C Part No.	DESCRIPTION
19738D	Rear wheel tire (8″).
19747D	Rear wheel spoke.
19954D	Rear wheel, complete (8″).
20256D	Rear wheel hub.

8″ OFFSET REAR WHEEL ATTACHMENT (20473D) (Special)

I H C Part No.	DESCRIPTION
20469D	Offset rear wheel tire (8″).
20470D	Offset rear wheel spoke, inner.
20471D	Offset rear wheel spoke, outer.
20472D	Offset rear wheel tire brace.
20474D	Offset rear wheel, complete (8″).

6″ EXTENSION TIRE ATTACHMENT (20467D) (Special)

I H C Part No.	DESCRIPTION
10743D	Rear wheel extension tire.
12346DA	Rear wheel extension tire fastening plate.

REAR WHEEL FENDER ATTACHMENT (20546D) (Special)

I H C Part No.	DESCRIPTION
20547D	Rear wheel fender, L. H.
20547DX	Rear wheel fender, L. H., complete with braces.
20548D	Rear wheel fender, R. H.
20548DX	Rear wheel fender, R. H., complete with braces.
20549D	Fender front brace, L. H.
20550D	Fender front brace, R. H.
20551D	Fender center brace, L. H.
20552D	Fender center brace, R. H.
20553D	Fender rear brace, L. H.
20554D	Fender rear brace, R. H.

COUNTERSHAFT BRAKE

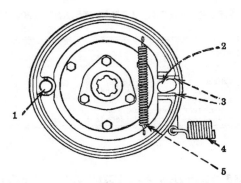

Illustration No. 75—Countershaft brake.

Ref. No.	I H C Part No.	DESCRIPTION
1	19743DX	Shoe pin, complete.
2	19756D	Camshaft.
3	19740D	Shoe wearing plate.
4	19836D	Cable spring.
5	15199D	Shoe spring.

COUNTERSHAFT BRAKE DRUM

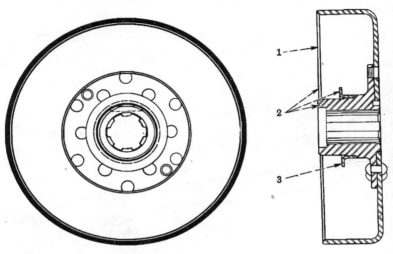

Illustration No. 76

Countershaft brake drum, complete (2248DX).

Ref. No.	IHC Part No.	DESCRIPTION
1	. . . .	Countershaft brake drum (order 2248DX).
2	2248DX	Countershaft brake drum and hub, complete.
3	20101D	Countershaft brake drum hub collar.

COUNTERSHAFT BRAKE SHEAVE ASSEMBLY

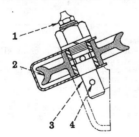

Illustration No. 77

Countershaft brake sheave assembly (sectional view).

Ref. No.	IHC Part No.	DESCRIPTION
1	14186D	Countershaft brake sheave shaft lubricator (Zerk).
2	1551DA	Countershaft brake sheave.
3	15134DB	Countershaft brake sheave shaft.
4	G 1119	Countershaft brake sheave shaft pin ($\frac{3}{16}$ x $1\frac{1}{4}$").

SEAT SUPPORT

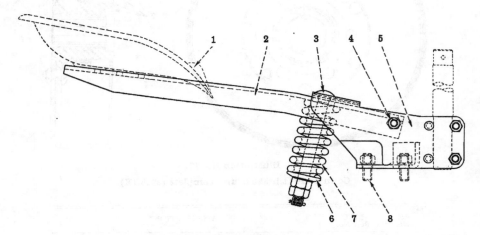

Illustration No. 78

Seat support assembly (sectional view).

Ref. No.	I H C Part No.	DESCRIPTION
1	MB488B	Seat.
2	19877D	Seat support (3″, 5-lb. channel).
3	10026DA	Seat support bolt ($\frac{3}{4}$ x $7\frac{1}{2}$″).
4	17387D	Seat support bracket bolt ($\frac{1}{2}$ x $4\frac{1}{2}$″).
5	19160D	Seat support bracket.
6	10027DA	Seat spring washer.
7	10214DA	Spring.
8	17388D	Seat support stud ($\frac{5}{8}$ x 2″).

REAR END OF TRACTOR

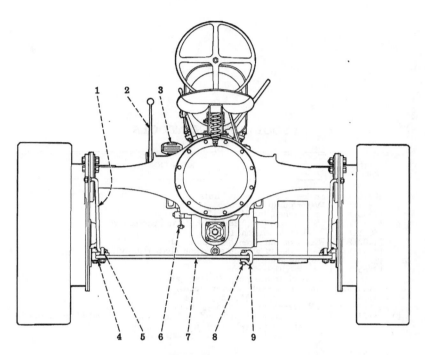

Illustration No. 79

Rear end of Tractor.

Ref. No.	I H C Part No.	DESCRIPTION
1	19849D	Drawbar brace.
2	2253D	Countershaft brake hand lever.
3	19846DX	Clutch pedal, complete.
4	1538DB	Drawbar hinge, R. H.
	1539DB	Drawbar hinge, L. H.
5	19851D	Drawbar adjusting rod eye-bolt.
6	19843DA	Clutch shifter rod.
7	19850D ·	Drawbar.
8	4558TM	Drawbar clevis pin (¾ x 4″).
9	6740TMA	Drawbar clevis.

TOOL BOX AND TOOLS

I H C Part No.	DESCRIPTION
10720D	Socket wrench, for $\frac{9}{16}$″ nuts.
11858D	Water pump wrench.
12335D	"S" wrench, for $\frac{3}{8}$″ and $\frac{1}{2}$″ nuts.
12737D	"S" wrench, for $\frac{1}{4}$″ and $\frac{5}{16}$″ nuts and cap screws.
13071D	Adjustable wrench, 12″.
14402D	Rear axle nut wrench (Export only).
14403D	Rear axle nut wrench extension (Export only).
15226D	Packing gland wrench.
19865D	Tool box (less cover).
20450D	Valve clearance gauge (tappet gauge).
E4A-289-X	Magneto wrench (with magneto).
G 3170	"S" wrench, for $\frac{5}{8}$″ and $\frac{3}{4}$″ nuts.
G 3172	"S" wrench, for $\frac{5}{16}$″ and $\frac{7}{16}$″ nuts.
G 3173	"S" wrench, for $\frac{1}{4}$″ nuts and cap screws, and $\frac{7}{16}$″ and $\frac{3}{8}$″ set screws.
G 3525	"S" wrench, for $\frac{7}{16}$″ and $\frac{1}{2}$″ nuts.
G 3526	"S" wrench, for $\frac{5}{8}$″ nuts and $\frac{3}{4}$″ cap screws.
G 8899	Punch.
H 758M	Cold chisel.
H 59599	Compressor (Zerk Model Z3A).
2587T	Gas pliers, 8″.
2588T	Screw driver, 5″.
7695TM	Oil can, coppered (4″ diam., 3″ high, 5″ bent spout).
13095V	Spark plug wrench.

D

D

E

IHC Part No.	Page	IHC Part No.	Page	IHC Part No.	Page	IHC Part No.	Page
		19850D	101	19963D	65	20547D	97
		19851D	101	19965D	95	20547DX	97
		19852D	81, 85	19966D	95	20548D	97
		19853D	81	19967D	63	20548DX	97
		19854D	81	19968D	79	20549D	97
		19855DX	81	19969D	87	20550D	97
19776D	87	19856D	90	19981D	69	20551D	97
19778D	85	19858D	81	19982D	58	20552D	97
19779DA	85, 87	19859D	81	20000D	69	20553D	97
19780D	85	19860D	81, 85	20032D	87	20554D	97
19781D	85	19861D	81, 85	20035D	71	20584D	61
19782D	85	19862D	81	20044D	67	20585D	61
19783D	53	19863D	63	20053D	67	20586D	61
19784D	85	19864D	53	20058D	67	20588D	65
19785D	87	19865D	53, 102	20060D	67	20590D	57
19786D	85	19866D	95	20073D	58	20601D	53, 71
19787D	85	19867D	59	20074D	58	20602DX	53, 79
19788D	87	19870D	59	20075D	63	20605DX	91, 93
19790D	87	19871D	53, 79	20101D	96, 99	20667D	65
19791D	87	19872DX	53, 79	20105D	85	20682DX	72
19793D	85	19874D	53	20106DX	93	21200D	67
19794D	85	19875D	63	20152D	58	21201D	67
19795D	85	19877D	53, 100	20154D	93	21202D	67
19796D	85	19878D	53	20155D	63	21203D	67
19797D	90	19879DX	53	20158D	83	21204D	67
19798D	85	19882D	53, 93	20167DX	71	21205D	67
19799D	85, 89	19883D	53	20168D	87	21206D	67
19800D	87, 90	19884D	53	20174D	95	21207D	67
19801D	87	19885DX	53, 79	20175DA	53, 96	21208D	67
19802D	87, 96	19886D	89	20203D	67	21209D	67
19804DA	87	19887D	89	20216D	96	21210D	67
19805D	87	19888D	89	20242D	67	21211D	67
19807D	87	19890DX	89	20246D	59	21212D	67
19808D	87	19891D	89	20256D	95, 97	21213D	67
19809D	87	19892D	89	20273D	55	21214D	67
19810D	87	19893DX	89	20274D	85	21215D	67
19811D	85	19894D	89	20279D	55	21216D	67
19812D	87	19895D	89	20284D	93	21217D	67
19813D	87	19896D	89	20288D	61	21218D	67
19815D	85	19897D	89	20289D	61	21220D	67
19816D	85	19898DX	57	20290D	61	21221D	67
19817D	85	19899D	59	20293D	61	21222D	67
19818D	85	19900D	59	20296D	61	21223D	67
19819D	85	19901D	59	20297D	61	21224D	67
19820D	85	19902D	59	20298DA	61	21225D	67
19821D	85	19903DX	57	20299D	61	21226D	67
19822D	85	19904D	55	20300D	61	21227D	67
19823D	87	19905D	55	20301D	61	21228D	67
19824D	87	19906D	65	20302DA	61	21229D	67
19825D	85	19907D	65	20303D	61	21231D	67
19826D	85	19908D	65	20304D	61	21232D	67
19828DX	96	19909D	65	20305DX	61	21233D	67
19829D	96	19911D	65	20306DX	61	21234D	67
19830D	90	19912D	65	20308D	61	21235D	67
19831D	85, 90	19915D	61	20312D	58	21236D	67
19832DX	53	19916D	62	20324D	58	21275D	69
19833D	96	19917D	62	20327D	69	21288D	73
19834D	96	19918DA	62	20328D	58, 69	21289D	73
19835D	96	19919D	83	20329D	58	21290D	73
19836D	53, 98	19920D	83	20374D	61	21291D	73
19839D	63	19921D	83	20450D	102		
19840D	53	19925DX	63	20469D	97		
19841D	63	19926D	53, 81	20470D	97		
19843DA	101	19931D	59	20471D	97		
19844DX	95	19953D	58, 83	20472D	97	**E**	
19846DX	101	19954D	97	20474D	97		
19847D	87	19960D	87	20504D	93		
19848D	53	19961D	87	20505D	58	E4 -1	75
19849D	101	19962D	59, 65	20510D	58	E4A-5AX	75

TABLE

SHOWING HOW TO CONVERT "INCHES" INTO MILLIMETERS

INCHES		METRIC
1 Inch (")	=	25,4 mm
1 Foot (') or 12 Inches	=	304,8 mm
$39\frac{3}{8}$ Inches	=	1 Meter

INCHES   MILLIMETERS

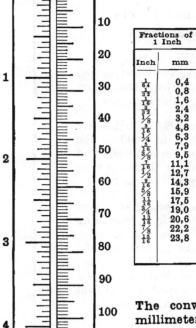

Fractions of 1 Inch	
Inch	mm
$\frac{1}{64}$	0,4
$\frac{1}{32}$	0,8
$\frac{1}{16}$	1,6
$\frac{3}{32}$	2,4
$\frac{1}{8}$	3,2
$\frac{3}{16}$	4,8
$\frac{1}{4}$	6,3
$\frac{5}{16}$	7,9
$\frac{3}{8}$	9,5
$\frac{7}{16}$	11,1
$\frac{1}{2}$	12,7
$\frac{9}{16}$	14,3
$\frac{5}{8}$	15,9
$\frac{11}{16}$	17,5
$\frac{3}{4}$	19,0
$\frac{13}{16}$	20,6
$\frac{7}{8}$	22,2
$\frac{15}{16}$	23,8

		Full Inches			
Inches	mm	Inches	mm	Inches	mm
1	25,4	21	533,4	41	1041,4
2	50,8	22	558,8	42	1066,8
3	76,2	23	584,2	43	1092,2
4	101,6	24	609,6	44	1117,6
5	127,0	25	635,0	45	1143,0
6	152,4	26	660,4	46	1168,4
7	177,8	27	685,8	47	1193,8
8	203,2	28	711,2	48	1219,2
9	228,6	29	736,6	49	1244,6
10	254,0	30	762,0	50	1270,0
11	279,4	31	787,4	51	1295,4
12	304,8	32	812,8	52	1320,8
13	330,2	33	838,2	53	1346,2
14	355,6	34	863,6	54	1371,6
15	381,0	35	889,0	55	1397,0
16	406,4	36	914,4	56	1422,4
17	431,8	37	939,8	57	1447,8
18	457,2	38	965,2	58	1473,2
19	482,6	39	990,6	59	1498,6
20	508,0	40	1016,0	60	1524,0

The conversion of lengths from inches into millimeters can be made by simple addition. For example, a certain part is $10\frac{15}{16}$" long:

$$10" \quad = 254,0 \text{ mm}$$
$$\tfrac{15}{16}" = 23,8 \text{ mm}$$
$$\text{Total } 10\tfrac{15}{16}" = 277,8 \text{ mm}$$

Conversion table as shown above is not figured up to the $\frac{1}{100}$ mm, but will prove sufficient for measurements as contained in this book.

Order Genuine Parts
for Replacements

Satisfactory and efficient service is endangered by purchasing imitation repairs, as cheap parts invariably mean short life and high cost.

Spare parts supplied for I H C Tractors are identical with those used in building the Tractor, and accurate workmanship and manufacturing equipment of the latest type insure interchangeability and proper fit.

If parts could be manufactured at a lower cost and sold at lower prices without sacrificing International quality, this would be done. The right material for the purpose and the knowledge acquired through more than twenty years of Tractor building enables International to produce quality that will not be found in the imitation repairs.

Remember that International Harvester Tractors deserve genuine International parts.

CPSIA information can be obtained
at www.ICGtesting.com
Printed in the USA
BVHW01s1402190918
527949BV00005B/38/P